The Children Who Found Christmas

Joshua Rhoades

Published by Joshua Paul Rhoades, 2024.

THE CHILDREN WHO FOUND CHRISTMAS

First edition. November 22, 2024.

ISBN: 979-8230751137

Written by Joshua Rhoades.

Also by Joshua Rhoades

A Life of Service
When Faith Rolls Up It's Sleeves
Love That Walks The Extra Mile
When Hope Feels Heavy, But Still Holds On

Leadership Series
The Law Of Vision Seeing Beyond The Horizon

The Law of
The Law of Communication Words That Build Or Break

The Old Paths
Seek The Old Paths Reviving Biblical Convictions

Standalone
Courage Under Fire: David's Stand On The Battlefield
Jonah's Journey: Voices Of Redemption And Lessons In Obedience
The Furnace Of Faith: 12 Principles From The Heat Of Faith
Whispers of Hope: Inspiring Stories of Men's Prayers In Scripture

Frontier Legends: The Oregon Dream
Elijah: A Beacon Of Boldness
HOOK, LINE & SAVIOUR - Faith Reflections from Fishing
Driven By Faith: Motor Racing Inspired Christian Life
30 Day Devotional - Bold and Strong- Coffee Devotions for a Courageous Christian Walk
Authentic Christianity: The Heart of Old Time Religion
Consider The Ant - God's Tiny Preachers
Flee Fornication: The Plea For Purity
Renewed Hope- How to Find Encouragement in God
Sounding The Call - The Voice of Conviction
The Altar - Where Heaven Meets Earth
The Bible's Battlefields- Timeless Lessons from Ancient Wars
The Sacred Art of Silence - How Silence Speaks in Scripture
Under Fire- The Sanctity of the Traditional Biblical Home
Who Is on the Lord's Side? A Call to Righteousness
What Is Truth? - From Skepticism to Submission
First and Goal- Faith and Football Fundamentals
From Dugout to Devotion- Spiritual Lessons from Baseball
Par for the Course- Faith and Fairways
The Believer's Pace- Tools for Running Life's Marathon
The Immutable Fortress- Security in God's Unchanging Nature
Biblical Bravery
Deer Stands and Devotions: A Hunter's Walk with God
Jesus Knows- Our Hearts, Our Responsibility
Restoration - Setting The Bone
Spiritual 911- God's Word for Life's Emergency's
The Freedom of Forgiveness
The Jezebel Effect - Ancient Manipulations Modern Lessons
The Shout That Stopped The Saviour
The Time Machine Chronicles: Old Testament Characters
Anchored In Truth Exploring The Depths of Psalm 119
Biblical Counsel on Anger
Proverbs' Portraits The Men God Mentions
Stumbling in the Dark - The Dangers of Alcohol

Guarding the Wicket Protecting Your Faith and Game

The Champion's Faith - Wrestling and Achieving Spiritual Victory

Scriptural Commands for Modern Times Living God's Word Today Volume 1

Scriptural Commands for Modern Times Living God's Word Today Volume 2

Scriptural Commands for Modern Times Living God's Word TodayVolume3

The Greatest Gift

A Christmas Journey of Faith

Daughter Of The King: Embracing Your Identity In Christ

Determination and Dedication Building Strong Faith As A Young Man

Walking Through Walls God's Power to Part the Storms of Life

David's Song Of Deliverance Praising God Through Every Storm

From Weakness to Warrior: Gideon's Transformation

Why Did Jesus Weep?

Living For God The Call To Be A Living Sacrifice

My Mind Is In A Fog What Do I Do?

Turning The Page Written By Grace

The Calling and Greatness of John the Baptist

For Such a Time Esther's Courageous Stand

From Brokenness To Beauty Written By The Pen of Grace

The Ultimate Guide to Massive Action- From Plans to Reality

A Heart Of Conviction

Serving In The Shadows

Repentance Revealed The Road Back To God

The Chief Sinner Meets The Chief Saviour Reflections On I Timothy 1:15

Answer The Call - 31 Days of Biblical Action

The Birthmark of the Believer

Reflections on Calvary's Cross

The Kingdom Builder Paul's Bold Proclamation of Christ

The Animal Of Pride

The Reach That Restores Christ Love For The Broken

Paul- The Many Roles of a Servant of Christ

Unshakeable Faith- 31 Days of Peace in God's Word

O Come, Let Us Adore Him- A Christmas Devotional

The Shepherd's Voice

The Trail From Vision To Mission

Enabled- Living God's Purpose With Power
Held Back But Not Defeated
The Enoch Walk
The Power and Precision of God's Word
The Children Who Found Christmas
Hearts of Valor - Faithful in the Call
Why It Matters Finding Hope in Moments of Frustration
The Wild West Lives On McCall Family Adventures
Igniting Courage Fueling Your Heart To Serve The Lord
The Characters of Christmas
When Jealousy Takes Aim
Fan The Flame
Faith Comes By Hearing
Intentional Love A 31-Day Devotional on Courtship
The Anointing A Shepherd's Touch Of Grace
Unveiling God's Masterpiece The Indestructible Word of God
Heart Strings of Scripture
The War Cry Of A Conqueror
The Law of Accountability The Measure Of A Leader
The Law of Adaptability Thriving Through Change and Challenge
The Poetry Of Us
Send Me Embracing the Call No Matter the Cost
Until All Have Heard

Dedication

To you, dear reader,

This book is for the seeker in your heart, the dreamer in your soul, and the child within who still believes in the magic of Christmas. It's for those who wonder if there's something more to the twinkling lights, wrapped gifts, and familiar carols—something deeper that touches the very core of who we are.

May this story meet you in the quiet moments, when the world outside seems loud and overwhelming, and remind you of the beauty found in simplicity. May it draw you into the warmth of faith, the wonder of hope, and the everlasting truth of God's love.

Whether you are reading this alone or sharing it with loved ones, my prayer is that these pages stir your heart to rediscover the miracle of Christmas—not just as a season but as a living story that continues to unfold in your life.

This book is a journey, and you are invited to walk alongside Abby, Luke, Sarah, and Jonah as they learn that Christmas isn't about perfection or performance—it's about a Savior who came to bring light into the darkness and love into every heart willing to receive it.

As you turn each page, may you find not only the story of Christmas but your own place within it. And may you always remember that the greatest gift has already been given, a gift meant for you: Jesus, the light of the world.

With hope and joy,
Joshua Rhoades

"For unto you is born this day in the city of David a Saviour, which is Christ the Lord."

– Luke 2:11

"Amidst the wonder of that holy night, the greatest gift was given—a gift that still calls to the hearts of all who seek Him."

Introduction

What is Christmas really about? That was the question the children set out to answer one snowy December. In their small town, Christmas was everywhere—twinkling lights hung from rooftops, decorated trees stood proudly in living room windows, and the scent of gingerbread seemed to drift through every street. But deep down, the four friends wondered if there was something more, something deeper than the carols, gifts, and decorations.

It all began on a quiet Christmas Eve, in the warm glow of their grandfather's living room. The fire crackled in the hearth, casting dancing shadows on the walls, while outside, snow blanketed the countryside in a hushed stillness. Grandpa James, with his silver hair and twinkling blue eyes, sat in his favorite chair, holding a Bible that looked as old as the stories he told. "Tonight," he said with a gentle smile, "I'm going to share the greatest story ever told—a story about how Christmas began, long before Bethlehem."

With those words, the children's journey into the heart of Christmas began. Over the next 31 days, the children learned about the amazing story of Jesus' birth. They discovered how the prophet Isaiah spoke of a Savior who would come to rescue the world, calling Him Immanuel, which means "God with us." They imagined Mary's courage when the angel Gabriel told her she would carry the Son of God and Joseph's faith as he trusted God's plan, even when it was hard to understand.

The children walked with Mary and Joseph through the dusty streets of Bethlehem and pictured the humble stable where Jesus was born. They marveled at how the King of Kings wasn't born in a palace but laid in a manger, showing that God's love is for everyone. They celebrated with the shepherds who heard the angels' joyful announcement and followed the wise men who traveled far, guided by a star, to bring gifts to the newborn King.

As they learned about these moments, the children began to see that Christmas wasn't just about what happened long ago—it was about what God was still doing today. They realized that the story of Christmas didn't end in the stable; it was the beginning of God's plan to bring hope, peace, and love to the world. They discovered that Jesus is the greatest gift ever given and that His light continues to shine in the hearts of those who believe.

Through the stories their grandfather shared, the children found Christmas—not just in the decorations, music, and traditions they loved, but in the deep, unshakable truth of God's love. This book invites you to join them on their journey of discovery. Each chapter is a new piece of the Christmas story, filled with wonder, hope, and joy. Whether you're a child or just young at heart, you'll find something to inspire and remind you of the true meaning of Christmas.

So come along and rediscover Christmas with the Abby, Luke Sarah, and Jonah. Together, you'll learn that Christmas isn't just a holiday—it's a story that's still unfolding, inviting everyone to take part. This is the story of "The Children Who Found Christmas." Let's begin.

Day 1 - The Prophecy Foretold

The fire crackled warmly in the stone hearth, casting long, flickering shadows across the walls of Abby's grandfather's cozy living room. It was Christmas Eve, and a deep hush had settled over the countryside, broken only by the occasional gust of wind rattling the windows. Outside, snow blanketed the world in a pristine white stillness, but inside, the room glowed with golden light. The faint scent of pine from the Christmas tree mingled with the aroma of spiced cider warming on the stove.

Abby sat cross-legged on the thick braided rug, her younger brother, Luke, sprawled beside her. Their cousins, Sarah and Jonah, perched on a low ottoman, their faces lit with anticipation. It was a family tradition, this gathering around Grandpa's big armchair, to hear him tell stories from the Bible that connected the Christmas season to something far bigger than just gifts and garlands.

Grandpa James, with his silver hair and twinkling blue eyes, sat with a thick old Bible resting on his lap. Its leather cover was worn smooth by years of use, and its gilded edges glinted in the firelight. He cleared his throat, his voice rich and steady, filling the room like a melody.

"Tonight," he began, "I want to tell you about something wonderful—something promised long before that night in Bethlehem. It's a story about hope, about waiting, and about the incredible way God keeps His promises."

The children leaned forward, their eyes fixed on their grandfather.

"Have you ever heard of the prophet Isaiah?" Grandpa asked.

Luke squirmed excitedly. "Wasn't he one of the guys who talked to God and told people what God said?"

"Exactly," Grandpa replied, a smile tugging at his lips. "Isaiah lived hundreds of years before Jesus was born, but God gave him messages about the future—messages that pointed to a Savior who would come to rescue the world."

He opened the Bible to a marked page and traced his finger along the verses, his voice quiet but commanding. "Isaiah said this: 'Therefore the Lord himself shall give you a sign; Behold, a virgin shall conceive, and bear a son, and shall call his name Immanuel.'"

Abby tilted her head. "Immanuel? What does that mean?"

Grandpa's eyes gleamed as he answered, "Immanuel means 'God with us.' It was a promise that one day, God Himself would come and dwell among His people—not as a distant king or a voice from the heavens, but as a person who would walk beside us, know our sorrows, and show us His love in the most personal way."

The room grew quiet as the children pondered this. Even the fire seemed to burn a little softer, as if it, too, were listening.

"But there's more," Grandpa continued, flipping a few pages. "In another part of Isaiah's prophecy, he says this: 'For unto us a child is born, unto us a son is given: and the government shall be upon his shoulder: and his name shall be called Wonderful, Counsellor, The mighty God, The everlasting Father, The Prince of Peace.'"

Jonah's brow furrowed in thought. "But Grandpa," he said slowly, "how did Isaiah know all that? It sounds like he was describing Jesus, but Jesus wasn't born yet."

Grandpa nodded. "You're right, Jonah. Jesus wasn't born yet—not for many, many years. But Isaiah didn't come up with these words on his own. God revealed them to him. You see, God wanted His people to know that He had a plan—a perfect plan to save them. Even when they felt lost or forgotten, God was preparing something wonderful."

He leaned forward, his voice lowering to a reverent whisper. "Imagine this: the people of Israel were waiting for this promise to come true for centuries. They passed down Isaiah's words from generation to generation, holding onto the hope that one day, a Savior would come. And then, on a quiet night in Bethlehem, in the humblest of places, it happened."

Abby clasped her hands, her eyes wide. "When Mary had baby Jesus?"

"That's right," Grandpa said, his face softening with a smile. "When Jesus was born, it wasn't just a beautiful story about a baby in a manger. It was the fulfillment of everything God had promised through Isaiah and so many others. God kept His word, just as He always does."

"But why did He do it that way?" Sarah asked, her voice barely above a whisper. "Why not send Jesus as a king in a palace?"

Grandpa's gaze rested on Sarah, and he nodded slowly. "That's a good question, Sarah. Jesus came not to rule with power and riches, but to show us a different kind of kingdom—one built on love, mercy, and grace. By being born in a stable, He showed us that God's love is for everyone, from the poorest shepherd to the richest king."

Luke's voice broke the quiet. "So, Jesus was like the Prince of Peace Isaiah talked about?"

"Exactly," Grandpa said, his smile deepening. "Jesus came to bring peace—not just the kind that means no fighting, but the kind of peace that fills our hearts and makes us whole. He came to heal what was broken, to forgive what was wrong, and to bring us back to God."

For a moment, the only sound was the soft crackle of the fire. Abby felt a warm glow inside her chest, as if the words her grandfather spoke were lighting something bright and unshakable within her.

"Do you see now," Grandpa asked, "why we celebrate Christmas the way we do? It's not just about presents or pretty decorations. It's about remembering the incredible gift God gave us—His Son, born to be our Savior. Jesus is the reason for our joy, our hope, and our peace."

The children nodded, their young faces glowing with newfound understanding.

Grandpa closed the Bible gently and rested it on the table beside him. He looked at each of them in turn, his eyes filled with love. "And just as God kept His promise to send a Savior, He promises to be with us always. That's what Immanuel means. God is with us—right here, right now."

As the fire burned low and the night deepened, the children sat quietly, their hearts full. Abby reached for Luke's hand, giving it a small squeeze. She didn't need to say anything; the look in her eyes said it all.

The story of Isaiah's prophecy and the birth of Jesus was no longer just words on a page or something recited in church. It was real, alive, and more wonderful than she had ever imagined.

And as the snow fell softly outside, Abby whispered a quiet prayer of thanks. For in that moment, she knew: the prophecy had been foretold, the promise fulfilled, and the Prince of Peace had come to be with them all.

Day 2 - God's Perfect Plan

The church sanctuary was quiet, save for the soft hum of whispers among the children as they shuffled to their seats. It was a chilly December evening, and the faint smell of pine and candle wax filled the air. Rows of garlands adorned the pews, and a massive nativity scene stood in one corner, its tiny figures bathed in the warm glow of string lights.

Abby, Luke, Sarah, and Jonah were among the group of children who had gathered for the special Christmas story hour. Pastor John had promised to tell them something extraordinary about God's perfect plan, and the anticipation was electric.

Pastor John was a kind man with silver hair and a booming laugh that made even the shyest children feel at home. Tonight, though, his demeanor was calm and reverent as he stepped to the front of the room. His Bible rested on the podium, and he began by surveying the children with a warm, gentle smile.

"Do you know what the word 'plan' means?" Pastor John asked, his voice carrying through the room.

Several hands shot up. Abby was first. "It's when you think about what you're going to do before you do it."

"Very good!" Pastor John replied, nodding. "A plan means knowing what you want to happen and figuring out the steps to make it so. Now, let me ask you this—do you think God has plans?"

The children nodded eagerly.

"That's right," Pastor John said, his voice taking on a thoughtful tone. "In fact, God's plans are unlike anything we could ever imagine. They're perfect. And one of the most incredible things about God's plan was how He prepared for the birth of Jesus—His Son—long before it happened."

The room grew quieter as Pastor John opened his Bible. The firelight from the sanctuary's Advent candles flickered across the room, reflecting in the children's wide eyes. He turned to a well-worn page and began to read.

"'For I know the thoughts that I think toward you, saith the Lord, thoughts of peace, and not of evil, to give you an expected end.'" He closed the Bible softly and looked up. "That's Jeremiah 29:11, a verse that reminds us God has plans for every single one of us. And it's also a reminder that His plans are always for good—even when they might not make sense at first."

Abby raised her hand, her voice hesitant but curious. "But Pastor John, how did God have a plan for Jesus? I thought Mary and Joseph didn't even know until the angel told them."

"Ah," Pastor John said, leaning slightly on the podium, "that's the beautiful part of God's perfect plan. Let me tell you a story."

He stepped down from the stage and walked closer to the children, his voice becoming soft, almost like a storyteller weaving a tale.

"Long before Mary and Joseph were even born, God had a plan to send His Son into the world to save us. Do you remember how the prophets in the Old Testament spoke about a Savior who would come? Isaiah, for example, told us that a virgin would conceive and bear a son, and His name would be called Immanuel, which means 'God with us.' That was part of God's plan."

The children nodded; they remembered Grandpa James telling them this story just the night before.

"But God's plan didn't stop there," Pastor John continued. "Even the small details of Jesus' birth were carefully prepared. Think about this: Jesus was born in Bethlehem. That wasn't by accident. Hundreds of years earlier, another prophet named Micah said, 'But thou, Bethlehem Ephratah, though thou be little among the thousands of Judah, yet out of thee shall he come forth unto me that is to be ruler in Israel.' Isn't that amazing? God planned for His Son to be born in Bethlehem long before it happened."

Jonah's eyes widened. "But Mary and Joseph lived in Nazareth. How did they end up in Bethlehem?"

"That's a great question, Jonah," Pastor John said, his eyes sparkling with approval. "And here's where we see God's perfect plan in action. At just the right time, the Roman emperor, Caesar Augustus, decided to take a census. That meant everyone had to travel back to their ancestral towns to be counted.

Joseph was from Bethlehem because he was a descendant of King David, so he and Mary had to make the journey."

Luke's hand shot up. "But wasn't Mary pregnant? That must've been really hard!"

"It was," Pastor John agreed, his tone filled with empathy. "Mary was about to have baby Jesus, and the journey to Bethlehem wasn't easy. But they made it because God's plan never fails. And when they got there, something else incredible happened. Does anyone know what it was?"

"The inn was full!" Sarah blurted out, unable to contain herself.

"Exactly," Pastor John said with a chuckle. "There was no room for them at the inn, so Jesus was born in a stable—a place where animals were kept. Think about that for a moment. The King of Kings wasn't born in a palace. He wasn't surrounded by wealth or comfort. Instead, He came into the world in the humblest of places. And do you know why?"

The children shook their heads.

"Because God's plan was to show us that His love isn't just for the rich or the powerful," Pastor John explained. "It's for everyone—shepherds, fishermen, farmers, and even little children like you."

Abby's face lit up with understanding. "That's why the angels told the shepherds first, isn't it? Because God's love is for everyone!"

"Exactly," Pastor John said, smiling warmly. "The shepherds were the first to hear the good news because Jesus came for people from all walks of life. God's perfect plan included everyone, no matter who they were or where they came from."

Pastor John paused, letting the weight of his words settle over the room. Then, he knelt down to the children's level, his voice soft but filled with conviction.

"Do you know what this means for us today? Just like God had a plan for Jesus' birth, He has a plan for each of you. Even when life feels uncertain or difficult, you can trust that God is working everything out for good. His plans for you are full of hope and love—just like His plan to send Jesus to be our Savior."

The children sat in thoughtful silence, their young minds trying to grasp the depth of what they'd heard. Abby felt a warm sense of reassurance wash over her. If God could plan something as amazing as Jesus' birth, surely He could take care of her, too.

Pastor John stood, his voice lifting once more. "As you celebrate Christmas this year, I want you to remember this: God's perfect plan is still unfolding. Just as He sent Jesus to show us His love, He's with us every day, guiding us and leading us closer to Him. And that, my friends, is the greatest gift of all."

The children clapped softly, their faces glowing with wonder. As the evening ended and they left the sanctuary, snow began to fall gently outside, blanketing the world in peace. Abby held Luke's hand tightly, her heart full of gratitude. God had a plan, and it was perfect.

Day 3 - Gabriel Visits Mary

The classroom buzzed with excitement as the Sunday school children gathered around the small stage. It was the second week of December, and anticipation for the Christmas play was at an all-time high. Strings of twinkling lights draped across the ceiling cast a warm glow, and the scent of pine wafted in from the fresh garlands decorating the windows.

Chloe stood nervously near the back of the room, clutching her script tightly. Her best friend, Emily, nudged her with an encouraging grin. "You're going to be amazing," Emily whispered. "You get to be Mary! That's the most important role."

"I know," Chloe replied, her voice a soft whisper. "But it's such a big part. What if I mess up?"

Emily shook her head. "You won't. You know the lines by heart. Besides, Mrs. Hendricks says the story is about more than just getting the words right. It's about understanding what it all means."

Chloe nodded, taking a deep breath. She had practiced every night for a week, standing in front of her bedroom mirror and imagining what it must have been like to hear Gabriel's words for the first time. Now, she just needed to channel that awe and wonder onto the little stage.

THE PLAY BEGAN WITH the narrators setting the scene, their voices clear and measured.

"In the sixth month, the angel Gabriel was sent from God unto a city of Galilee, named Nazareth," read Caleb, one of the older boys. His voice resonated in the small room, capturing the attention of the audience.

Chloe walked to the center of the stage, her long blue robe swishing softly against the wooden floor. She knelt beside a simple wooden bench meant to represent her home, mimicking the quiet tasks Mary might have been doing on that fateful day.

"And the angel came in unto her, and said, 'Hail, thou that art highly favoured, the Lord is with thee: blessed art thou among women,'" Caleb continued.

Chloe looked up as if startled, her expression shifting from confusion to awe as Emily, dressed in a shimmering white robe with gold accents, entered from stage left. Emily's costume sparkled under the lights, giving her an ethereal glow. She stretched out her hands in a gesture of peace, her smile gentle.

"Fear not, Mary," Emily said, her voice steady and melodic. "For thou hast found favour with God. And, behold, thou shalt conceive in thy womb, and bring forth a son, and shalt call his name Jesus."

Chloe gasped softly, her hands trembling as she pressed them to her chest. Her mind whirled as she imagined what Mary might have felt in that moment. How could someone like her—a simple girl from a small town—be chosen for something so miraculous? Chloe let those emotions wash over her as she delivered her next line.

"How shall this be, seeing I know not a man?" she asked, her voice tinged with both wonder and hesitance.

Emily stepped closer, her expression serene, embodying the divine messenger. "The Holy Ghost shall come upon thee, and the power of the Highest shall overshadow thee: therefore also that holy thing which shall be born of thee shall be called the Son of God. And behold, thy cousin Elisabeth, she hath also conceived a son in her old age: and this is the sixth month with her, who was called barren. For with God nothing shall be impossible."

The room seemed to hold its breath as Chloe processed the angel's words. She imagined Mary's heart pounding in her chest, her thoughts swirling with questions and fears. But then, like the warmth of the sun breaking through storm clouds, peace settled over her. She lowered her head slightly and spoke the words that would forever echo through history:

"Behold the handmaid of the Lord; be it unto me according to thy word."

AS THE PLAY CONTINUED, Chloe's mind wandered, lost in the story she was bringing to life. What must it have been like for Mary to receive such a message? The angel had spoken of a divine plan, one far beyond human understanding. Mary's faith and humility shone brightly, even in the face of uncertainty. Chloe marveled at the courage it must have taken for her to say yes.

The final scene of the play drew to a close with a song about Mary's obedience, and the audience erupted into applause. Chloe and Emily exchanged a look of relief and pride as they took their bows.

LATER THAT EVENING, Chloe sat by the fireplace in her living room, her thoughts still lingering on Mary's story. The Christmas tree twinkled nearby, its ornaments catching the warm light. Her parents were in the kitchen, preparing cocoa for everyone, but Chloe's heart was full of questions she wasn't sure how to ask.

Her grandmother, who had been watching the play from the front row, noticed the pensive look on Chloe's face. She sat down beside her and placed a gentle hand on her shoulder. "You were wonderful tonight, Chloe," she said softly. "You brought Mary to life in such a beautiful way."

"Thanks, Grandma," Chloe said, her voice barely above a whisper. She hesitated for a moment before continuing. "Can I ask you something?"

"Of course," her grandmother replied, her eyes kind.

"How do you think Mary felt when the angel told her everything? I mean, she must have been scared, right? It's such a big thing to be chosen by God for something like that."

Her grandmother nodded thoughtfully. "I imagine she was scared at first," she said. "After all, she was just a young girl, probably close to your age. But Mary had a deep faith in God. She trusted that if He had a plan for her, He would also give her the strength to fulfill it."

Chloe considered this, her eyes flickering to the flames dancing in the hearth. "Do you think God has plans like that for all of us?" she asked.

"Absolutely," her grandmother said, her voice filled with conviction. "The Bible tells us that God has a purpose for each of our lives. Sometimes His plans are big and obvious, like they were for Mary. Other times, they're quieter, but no less important. What matters is that we're willing to say yes to Him, just like Mary did."

Chloe smiled, her heart swelling with a sense of peace. She didn't know what God's plan for her life might be, but she felt certain that she wanted to trust Him, just as Mary had.

THAT NIGHT, AS CHLOE drifted off to sleep, she dreamed of shimmering angels and a star-filled sky over Bethlehem. She saw Mary, radiant with faith, cradling the Son of God in her arms. And in her heart, Chloe carried the truth that had been spoken to her so clearly that day: with God, nothing shall be impossible.

Day 4 - Mary's Faithful Yes

The late afternoon sun streamed through the windows of the church, painting golden patterns on the worn wooden pews. Ben sat in the back row, fidgeting with the zipper of his jacket. He wasn't sure why he felt uneasy. Christmas was supposed to be a happy time, filled with carols and decorations, but something about today's Sunday school lesson had left a knot in his chest.

Across the room, Miss Clara, their Sunday school teacher, stood at a small table covered with a red cloth. She had a kind smile and a way of making Bible stories feel real, as if you could almost step into the pages yourself. Today, she had talked about Mary—the young girl who had said "yes" to God's plan without hesitation. Ben hadn't been able to stop thinking about it.

"Okay, everyone," Miss Clara said, clapping her hands gently to get their attention. "Before we wrap up, let's talk about what we can learn from Mary's story. She was just a regular person, like you and me, but she trusted God completely. She said, 'Be it unto me according to thy word.' That's a pretty big deal, isn't it?"

Ben slouched lower in his seat, avoiding her gaze. He wasn't sure if he could ever be as brave as Mary. He wasn't even sure he understood what it meant to trust God like that.

AFTER CLASS, BEN STAYED behind as the other kids filed out. Miss Clara noticed him lingering and approached with a gentle smile. "Something on your mind, Ben?"

He shrugged, staring at the floor. "I don't know... I just don't get it. How could Mary say 'yes' so easily? What if she was scared? What if things didn't go the way she thought they would?"

Miss Clara pulled up a chair and sat beside him. "Those are great questions," she said. "And you know what? I think Mary probably was scared. She was young, maybe only a little older than you, and God was asking her to do something extraordinary. But here's the thing—Mary didn't say 'yes' because she had everything figured out. She said 'yes' because she trusted God."

Ben chewed on his lip, turning her words over in his mind. "But how could she trust Him that much?"

Miss Clara leaned back, her eyes thoughtful. "I think Mary trusted God because she believed in His promises. Remember what the angel told her? 'For with God, nothing shall be impossible.' Mary knew that God was faithful, that He always keeps His word. So even though she didn't know how everything would work out, she believed that God's plan was good."

Ben nodded slowly, but he still felt a tug of doubt in his heart. He thanked Miss Clara and headed home, her words echoing in his mind.

THAT EVENING, AS BEN sat on his bed, he stared out the window at the snow-covered street below. The world outside seemed so still, so quiet, as if it were holding its breath. On his nightstand, his Bible lay open to Luke 1, where Miss Clara had read from earlier.

He picked it up and scanned the passage again:

"And Mary said, Behold the handmaid of the Lord; be it unto me according to thy word."

Ben sighed, closing the book gently. He tried to imagine what it must have been like for Mary. The angel had appeared out of nowhere, telling her she would give birth to the Son of God. That wasn't just big news—it was life-changing. And yet, Mary had responded with humility and obedience, even though she didn't have all the answers.

What would it be like to trust God like that? Ben thought about his own life. He didn't have any angels showing up with big announcements, but he did have questions—lots of them. What if he wasn't good enough? What if he messed up? What if God had plans for him that he wasn't ready for?

He leaned back against his pillows, staring up at the ceiling. "God," he whispered, "how do I trust You like Mary did? I want to, but it's hard. What if I mess everything up?"

THE NEXT MORNING, BEN'S mom called him downstairs. "We're going to visit Grandma," she said, handing him his coat. "She wants help putting up her Christmas decorations."

Ben loved going to Grandma's house. It always smelled like cookies, and she had a way of making you feel like you were the most important person in the world. As they drove through the snowy streets, he gazed out the window, lost in thought. Maybe Grandma would have some advice. She always seemed to know the right thing to say.

When they arrived, Grandma greeted them with warm hugs and ushered Ben into the living room. Boxes of ornaments and tinsel were scattered everywhere, and the tree stood in the corner, waiting to be decorated.

"Ben, can you help me with the angel for the top of the tree?" Grandma asked, holding up a delicate porcelain figure.

Ben nodded and climbed onto a step stool to place the angel carefully at the top. As he did, he thought about Mary again. The angel Gabriel had brought her such a big, scary message, and she had still said yes.

"Grandma," Ben said, climbing down from the stool, "can I ask you something?"

"Of course, sweetheart," Grandma said, sitting down on the couch and patting the spot beside her.

"How do you trust God when you don't know what's going to happen?" Ben asked, his voice small.

Grandma's face softened, and she took his hand in hers. "Oh, Ben, that's a question we all ask at some point," she said. "The truth is, trusting God doesn't mean you won't ever feel scared or unsure. It just means you believe that He loves you and that His plans are good—even if you don't understand them right away."

Ben frowned. "But what if I mess up? What if I say yes to something, but then I can't do it?"

Grandma smiled, her eyes crinkling at the corners. "Do you know what's amazing about God, Ben? He doesn't expect us to be perfect. He just wants us to be willing. When Mary said 'yes,' she wasn't saying she had everything figured out. She was saying, 'God, I trust You to help me do what You've asked.' And He did."

Ben sat quietly, letting her words sink in. Maybe trusting God wasn't about having all the answers. Maybe it was about believing that God would be with him, no matter what.

THAT NIGHT, AS BEN lay in bed, he thought about Mary again. He imagined her sitting quietly in her home, hearing the angel's message and feeling her heart pound with fear and wonder. He imagined her looking up and saying, "Be it unto me according to thy word." It wasn't just bravery—it was faith.

Ben pulled his blanket up to his chin and whispered into the stillness of his room. "God, I don't know what You have planned for me, but I want to trust You. Help me to say yes, just like Mary did."

As he drifted off to sleep, a sense of peace settled over him, like a gentle whisper in his heart: With God, nothing shall be impossible.

5 - Joseph's Dream

The house smelled of pine and cinnamon, the scent wafting from the candle burning in the center of the dining table. Snow fell softly outside the window, muffling the sounds of the neighborhood as night settled in. Daniel sat cross-legged on the plush living room carpet, his little sister Lily beside him, surrounded by colorful paper and markers. They'd spent the afternoon drawing pictures of the nativity scene for their Sunday school class.

Daniel glanced at his dad, who was stirring a pot of hot cocoa in the kitchen. "Dad," Daniel called, holding up a lopsided drawing of a man standing beside a woman with a glowing halo. "Did Joseph really believe the angel when he came in a dream? What if he thought it wasn't real?"

His dad paused, wiping his hands on a dish towel, and turned to face Daniel. "That's a great question, buddy," he said, his voice warm and steady. "Joseph's story is one of incredible courage and faith. Do you want to hear it?"

Daniel nodded eagerly, and Lily scooted closer, her eyes wide. Their dad carried the cocoa mugs to the living room and sat down in his favorite armchair. The fire crackled softly in the hearth, casting flickering shadows across the walls as he opened his Bible to the book of Matthew.

"OKAY," DAD BEGAN, HIS tone settling into that of a storyteller. "Let's start from the beginning. Joseph was a carpenter—a hardworking, humble man who lived in a small town called Nazareth. He was engaged to a young woman named Mary, and they were probably very excited about their future together. But then, something happened that turned Joseph's world upside down."

Daniel leaned forward, his brow furrowed. "What happened?"

Dad looked at him, his expression serious yet kind. "Mary told Joseph that she was going to have a baby. But this wasn't just any baby—this was the Son of

God, conceived by the Holy Spirit. Now, imagine how Joseph must have felt. It didn't make sense. He might have felt confused, hurt, or even afraid. In those days, it was a big deal to be engaged, and for Mary to be pregnant before they were married—it would have been hard for Joseph to understand."

Lily's eyes widened. "Did Joseph get mad at Mary?"

Dad shook his head. "The Bible doesn't say Joseph got mad, but it does say he was a good man. He loved Mary, and he didn't want to hurt her. Even though he didn't understand what was happening, he decided to quietly break off the engagement so Mary wouldn't face shame or punishment."

Daniel frowned. "But if he was going to break it off, how did they end up staying together?"

Dad smiled knowingly and flipped to Matthew 1:20. "This is where the angel comes in," he said. "Joseph went to bed one night, probably with a heavy heart, and that's when God sent him a message in a dream. The angel said, 'Joseph, thou son of David, fear not to take unto thee Mary thy wife: for that which is conceived in her is of the Holy Ghost.'"

Lily gasped softly, her small hands clutching the edge of the rug. "What did Joseph do? Did he believe the angel?"

Dad's voice grew gentle as he continued. "The angel went on to explain that Mary's baby would save people from their sins. The angel even told Joseph what to name the child—Jesus, which means 'The Lord saves.' When Joseph woke up, he didn't hesitate. He obeyed what the angel had told him. He took Mary as his wife, and he cared for her and baby Jesus as God had asked."

THE ROOM WAS QUIET for a moment, the only sound the crackling of the fire. Daniel stared into the flames, imagining Joseph lying in bed, staring at the ceiling after the dream. He tried to picture what it must have been like to make such a big decision based on something that happened in a dream.

"Dad," Daniel said, breaking the silence, "wasn't Joseph scared? What if other people didn't believe him?"

Dad nodded. "I'm sure Joseph was scared," he said. "Doing what God asks isn't always easy, especially when it means people might not understand or agree with you. But Joseph trusted God. He knew that if God had a plan, it was a good one, even if it was hard to see how everything would work out. That's what faith is all about—trusting God even when you don't have all the answers."

"But what if Joseph had said no?" Lily asked, her voice small. "What if he didn't do what the angel said?"

Dad smiled gently at her. "That's a good question, Lily. God always gives us a choice, but He also gives us the strength to do what's right when we trust Him. Joseph chose to obey, and because of that, he got to be part of God's amazing plan to bring Jesus into the world."

LATER THAT EVENING, Daniel sat in his room, thinking about the story. His dad's words about courage and faith echoed in his mind. He thought about Joseph waking up from the dream, knowing what he had to do but not knowing how things would turn out. It made him wonder if he'd ever have to make a hard choice like that—one that required trusting God even when it was scary.

As Daniel climbed into bed, his dad came in to tuck him in. "Still thinking about Joseph?" Dad asked, sitting on the edge of the bed.

Daniel nodded. "I just don't get how he could be so sure. What if he had been wrong? What if the dream wasn't real?"

Dad placed a hand on Daniel's shoulder. "Sometimes, Daniel, faith means stepping out even when you're not 100% sure. It means trusting that God will guide you and help you do what's right. Joseph didn't have all the answers, but he had God's promise. And that was enough."

Daniel thought about this for a moment. "Do you think I'll ever have to trust God like that?"

"I think we all do, in different ways," Dad said with a smile. "It might not be as dramatic as an angel in a dream, but there will be times when you have to make a choice to trust God, even if it's hard. And when that time comes, remember Joseph's story. Remember that God's plans are always good, and He'll give you the courage you need."

AS THE SNOW FELL SOFTLY outside, Daniel drifted off to sleep, dreaming of angels and starlit skies. In his dream, he saw Joseph walking beside

Mary, his head held high, his heart full of trust. And when Daniel woke up the next morning, he felt a quiet sense of peace, knowing that just like Joseph, he could trust God to guide him through whatever lay ahead.

Day 6 - The Journey to Bethlehem

The snowstorm raged outside, battering against the windows of Abby and Ben's house. The two siblings were tucked under a cozy blanket on the couch, sipping hot cocoa as the flames from the fireplace crackled and popped. The living room was adorned with twinkling Christmas lights, and the faint sound of carols played from a speaker in the corner.

"Do you think Mary and Joseph ever had to deal with snowstorms?" Ben asked suddenly, his gaze fixed on the frosted window.

Abby chuckled, pulling the blanket tighter around her shoulders. "Probably not, Ben. It was warmer in Bethlehem, right? But it wasn't easy for them either. They didn't have cars or comfy couches."

Their dad, seated in his favorite armchair with a Bible resting on his lap, overheard the conversation and smiled. "That's a good question, Ben. No, Mary and Joseph didn't have to deal with snowstorms, but their journey to Bethlehem was challenging in other ways. Would you like me to tell you about it?"

Abby and Ben nodded eagerly, their attention now fully on their dad.

DAD LEANED FORWARD, his voice taking on the warm, engaging tone he used whenever he told stories. "It all started with a decree from Caesar Augustus. He was the ruler of the Roman Empire at the time, and he decided that everyone had to be counted in a census. That meant people had to travel to their ancestral towns to register. For Joseph, that meant a long trip to Bethlehem because he was from the family of King David."

"How far was it?" Abby asked, her brow furrowed.

Dad tapped his chin thoughtfully. "Well, Bethlehem was about 90 miles from Nazareth. That's like walking from here to the next big city. And remember, Mary was very close to giving birth to baby Jesus. Can you imagine how hard that must have been?"

Ben's eyes widened. "Did they have a donkey? Or did Mary have to walk the whole way?"

"It's possible they had a donkey," Dad said, "but the Bible doesn't specifically say. Either way, it would have been a slow, exhausting journey. The roads were rough, and they had to travel through hills and valleys. There weren't any hotels or restaurants, just little villages where they might find a place to rest."

Abby closed her eyes, trying to picture it. "Mary must have been so tired. I get tired just walking around the mall!"

Dad chuckled. "I'm sure she was. But Mary and Joseph kept going because they trusted that God had a plan. They didn't know everything that was going to happen, but they believed that God would take care of them."

"LET'S IMAGINE WHAT it was really like," Dad said, leaning back in his chair. "Close your eyes for a moment and picture it."

Abby and Ben obeyed, letting the room around them fade as their dad's words transported them back in time.

THE SUN HUNG LOW IN the sky, casting a golden glow over the rocky hillsides. Joseph adjusted the straps of his pack and glanced back at Mary, who was perched carefully on a donkey. She shifted slightly, one hand resting protectively on her rounded belly. The journey had been long—days of walking under the hot sun, stopping only when they found a shady spot or a small village where they could buy food and water.

"Are you all right, Mary?" Joseph asked, his voice full of concern.

Mary nodded, though her face was pale and tired. "I'm fine," she said softly. "Just a little longer, right?"

Joseph smiled, though he felt the weight of their situation pressing on his heart. "Just a little longer," he assured her, though he wasn't entirely sure how much farther they had to go. The road to Bethlehem was unpredictable, and they still had to climb a steep hill before reaching the city.

As they walked, the wind picked up, carrying with it the scent of dry earth and olive trees. The donkey stumbled slightly on the uneven path, and Joseph reached out to steady it.

"Thank you," Mary murmured, her voice barely audible.

They pressed on, the silence broken only by the crunch of their footsteps on the gravel. Occasionally, they passed other travelers—some with carts piled high with goods, others on foot like them, all making their way to their ancestral towns. Most offered only a brief nod or a murmured greeting before continuing on their way.

"I BET MARY FELT SCARED," Abby said, opening her eyes briefly. "I would be scared, traveling all that way and not knowing if there'd be a place to stay."

"She probably was scared," Dad agreed. "But she also had faith. Remember, the angel had told her that she would give birth to the Son of God. She knew that God wouldn't abandon her, even if the journey was hard."

AS THE SUN DIPPED BELOW the horizon, painting the sky in hues of orange and purple, Joseph spotted the flickering lights of Bethlehem in the distance. Relief washed over him, though he knew their journey wasn't over yet. The city was crowded—far more crowded than he had expected. People filled the narrow streets, talking loudly and carrying bundles of supplies.

"Do you think there's room for us?" Mary asked, her voice laced with hope and exhaustion.

Joseph glanced around, his heart sinking. Every inn they passed had a "No Vacancy" sign, and the innkeepers all shook their heads apologetically. "I'm sorry," one of them said. "There's no room left."

Desperation began to creep in, but Joseph refused to give up. He led Mary through the streets, asking at every door until finally, one kind innkeeper gestured toward a stable in the back.

"It's not much," the man said, "but it's clean, and you're welcome to use it."

Joseph thanked him, and together, he and Mary made their way to the stable. It was a simple structure, filled with the earthy smell of hay and the soft sounds of animals shifting in their stalls. Joseph laid out a bed of straw for Mary, and she sank onto it with a sigh of relief.

"This will do," she said, her voice steady despite her exhaustion. "God has brought us this far. He will see us through."

"I DON'T THINK I COULD do what Mary and Joseph did," Ben said, his eyes still closed. "It sounds so hard."

Dad's voice was gentle as he responded. "It was hard, Ben. But Mary and Joseph weren't alone. God was with them every step of the way, just like He's with us when we face challenges. They trusted Him, even when things didn't make sense, and He provided for them."

THE STABLE WAS QUIET as night fell, the stars shining brightly overhead. Mary and Joseph rested, their hearts full of both uncertainty and hope. They didn't know what the next hours or days would bring, but they clung to the promise that God had made—that the child Mary carried would be the Savior of the world.

ABBY OPENED HER EYES, the image of the stable still vivid in her mind. "I think I understand now," she said softly. "Mary and Joseph kept going because they knew God's plan was bigger than their problems."

"That's exactly right," Dad said, smiling. "The journey to Bethlehem wasn't easy, but it taught them—and us—about perseverance and trust. Sometimes, God asks us to do hard things, but He always gives us the strength to get through them."

Ben sat up, his face thoughtful. "So, when things get hard for us, we can remember Mary and Joseph and know that God is with us, too?"

Dad nodded. "That's right, Ben. Just like He guided Mary and Joseph to Bethlehem, He'll guide us through our own journeys. All we have to do is trust Him and keep moving forward."

As the snowstorm continued outside, Abby and Ben felt a warm sense of peace settle over them. The story of Mary and Joseph's journey had come alive in their hearts, reminding them that even in the hardest times, God's presence and promises are always there to light the way.

Day 7 - No Room at the Inn

The Sunday school classroom was quiet, the children sitting in a semi-circle around Miss Clara, who held a large illustrated Bible in her lap. Chloe was perched on the edge of her chair, her eyes fixed on the picture Miss Clara had just shown them—a weary Mary and Joseph standing before an innkeeper, his face apologetic as he gestured to a crowded courtyard. Chloe's heart tugged at the image of Mary, her hand resting protectively over her rounded belly, while Joseph's face carried the weight of desperation.

"And so," Miss Clara said, her voice warm and steady, "Mary and Joseph found no room at the inn. Instead, they were offered a place in a stable—a humble, quiet spot where the King of Kings would be born."

Chloe raised her hand, her brow furrowed. "Miss Clara, why didn't anyone let them in? I mean, it was baby Jesus! How could they say no?"

Miss Clara smiled kindly. "That's a good question, Chloe. Remember, the people in Bethlehem didn't know who Mary and Joseph were. The town was crowded because of the census, and everyone was busy finding places to stay. Sometimes, when life feels full and busy, it's easy to overlook what's truly important."

The class nodded thoughtfully, but Chloe felt a twinge of sadness in her chest. What if she had been in Bethlehem that night? Would she have made room for Jesus?

LATER THAT EVENING, Chloe sat in her room, a small nativity scene on her desk. She had arranged it carefully, placing the shepherds, wise men, and animals around Mary, Joseph, and baby Jesus in the manger. The soft glow of the Christmas lights on her wall reflected off the tiny porcelain figures. She traced her finger over the stable's roof, imagining the scene in Bethlehem on that first Christmas night.

Her mom peeked into the room, a warm smile on her face. "Thinking about today's lesson?" she asked.

Chloe nodded. "It just feels so unfair," she said, her voice small. "Mary and Joseph had nowhere to go, and no one let them in. Why didn't anyone care enough to help them?"

Her mom walked in and sat on the edge of Chloe's bed. "You know," she said gently, "I've thought about that story a lot, too. And it makes me wonder if the innkeepers weren't being mean—they just didn't have any space left. Their rooms were already full."

Chloe frowned, her mind turning over the thought. "But couldn't they have made room? Like, moved things around or squeezed in?"

Her mom chuckled softly. "Maybe. But think about how often our lives can get crowded, too. Sometimes, we're so busy with school, sports, or even fun things like Christmas shopping that we forget to make room for Jesus in our hearts."

THAT NIGHT, CHLOE LAY awake in her bed, staring at the twinkling lights on the ceiling. The idea of making room for Jesus swirled in her mind. She thought about her busy days, filled with homework, soccer practice, and time spent scrolling through videos on her tablet. Was her heart as crowded as those inns in Bethlehem?

The next morning, as the snow fell softly outside, Chloe found herself drawn back to the nativity scene on her desk. She imagined Mary and Joseph's journey, the crowded streets of Bethlehem, and the hurried voices of innkeepers explaining that there was no room.

She closed her eyes and let the scene unfold in her mind.

THE STREETS OF BETHLEHEM were alive with noise and activity. People bustled about, carrying bundles of belongings and leading donkeys laden with supplies. The inns were overflowing, their courtyards packed with travelers trying to secure a spot for the night.

Joseph's face was lined with exhaustion as he guided the donkey carrying Mary through the narrow streets. Mary held onto the donkey's reins, her breaths shallow and labored. The baby would be coming soon—she could feel it.

They approached another inn, and Joseph stepped forward, his voice steady but tinged with desperation. "Please," he said to the innkeeper. "My wife is about to have a baby. Do you have any room at all?"

The innkeeper shook his head, glancing at the crowded courtyard behind him. "I'm sorry," he said, his voice apologetic. "We're completely full. There's no space left."

Joseph looked back at Mary, his heart sinking. She met his gaze with a small, weary smile, her faith unshaken despite their circumstances. The innkeeper hesitated, then pointed toward a stable at the edge of the property.

"It's not much," he said, "but it's sheltered. You're welcome to stay there."

Joseph nodded, his gratitude evident. He led Mary to the stable, the soft glow of lanterns illuminating the humble space. The air was filled with the earthy scent of hay and the gentle sounds of animals shifting in their stalls. Joseph spread a blanket over a pile of straw, helping Mary settle onto the makeshift bed.

As the night deepened, the stars above Bethlehem shone brightly, one in particular casting a radiant light over the stable. It was here, in this quiet and humble place, that the Son of God would enter the world.

CHLOE OPENED HER EYES, her heart full as the imagined scene faded. She felt a deep sense of awe at the thought of Jesus being born in such a simple, ordinary setting. The King of Kings had come into the world not with fanfare or luxury, but with humility and grace.

AT BREAKFAST, CHLOE shared her thoughts with her mom. "I was thinking about Mary and Joseph last night," she said, her voice thoughtful. "I think the story isn't just about the inns being full. It's about how we can be like the innkeepers if we're not careful—too busy or distracted to make room for Jesus."

Her mom smiled, her eyes warm with pride. "That's a beautiful way to think about it, Chloe. Making room for Jesus in our hearts means putting Him first, even when life feels busy."

Chloe nodded, a quiet determination settling in her chest. She decided then and there that she wanted to make more room for Jesus—not just at Christmas, but every day.

LATER THAT DAY, CHLOE found ways to live out her decision. She set aside her tablet for a while and helped her mom bake cookies for their elderly neighbor, Mr. Davis. She read a chapter from her children's Bible, imagining the nativity story with fresh eyes. And when her little brother came into her room asking to play a game, she put down her markers and spent the next hour laughing with him over a board game.

As the sun set and the Christmas lights twinkled once again, Chloe felt a warmth in her heart that had nothing to do with the fire in the hearth. It was the quiet joy of knowing she was making room for Jesus.

THAT NIGHT, AS CHLOE lay in bed, she whispered a prayer into the stillness. "Jesus, I'm sorry for the times I've been too busy to think about You. Please help me to always make room for You in my heart."

And as she drifted off to sleep, she felt a sense of peace, knowing that her heart, unlike the crowded inns of Bethlehem, had a place for Him.

Day 8 - Jesus is Born

The fireplace crackled softly in the corner of the living room, its warmth wrapping around the group of children gathered on the thick rug. Abby's grandma, a woman with silver hair and kind eyes, sat in her rocking chair, the soft rhythm of its creak adding to the cozy atmosphere. She held a well-worn Bible on her lap, its pages edged with gold, and she glanced up with a gentle smile as the children whispered among themselves.

"Are you ready for the most important story of all?" Grandma asked, her voice warm and inviting.

"Yes!" came the chorus of replies, their eager faces turning toward her. Abby scooted closer, her hands clasped in anticipation, while her younger brother, Ben, leaned back against the couch, his gaze fixed on the Bible.

Grandma flipped to a marked page and smoothed it open. "This is the story of the night Jesus was born," she began. "The night that changed everything."

THE ROOM SEEMED TO grow quieter as Grandma's voice carried them back in time.

"Mary and Joseph had been traveling for days," she said. "The road to Bethlehem was long and rough, but they had no choice. Caesar Augustus, the Roman ruler, had declared that everyone must go to their ancestral towns to be counted. Joseph was from the family of King David, so they had to make the journey to Bethlehem."

The children listened intently as she continued. "Mary was expecting a baby—a very special baby. Do you remember what the angel told Mary about this child?"

Abby raised her hand, her voice soft but sure. "The angel said He would be the Son of God."

"That's right," Grandma said with a nod. "And so, even though the journey was hard, Mary and Joseph kept going. They trusted that God would take care of them."

GRANDMA'S WORDS PAINTED a vivid picture, and Abby closed her eyes, imagining the scene. She saw Mary and Joseph walking along a dusty path, the sun setting behind the hills. Mary rode on a donkey, her face tired but peaceful, while Joseph led the way, his steps steady and determined.

The streets of Bethlehem were crowded with people by the time they arrived. The noise of travelers filled the air—voices calling out, carts rattling over stones, and the braying of donkeys. Joseph stopped at the first inn they came to, knocking on the wooden door.

"Please," he said, his voice steady but urgent. "My wife is about to have a baby. Do you have a room?"

The innkeeper shook his head. "I'm sorry," he said. "We're full."

One by one, the doors of other inns closed with the same answer. No room. No space. The streets grew darker as night fell, and Joseph's heart grew heavier with each step. He looked back at Mary, her face pale and weary, and prayed silently for a solution.

Finally, one kind innkeeper paused, thinking. "I don't have a room," he said, "but there's a stable out back. It's not much, but it's sheltered."

Joseph looked at Mary, who nodded with a faint smile. "It will do," she said.

GRANDMA'S VOICE SOFTENED, drawing the children deeper into the story. "And so, they went to the stable—a simple place meant for animals, not for people. The air smelled of hay and earth, and the gentle sounds of cows and sheep filled the space. It wasn't a palace, but it was peaceful."

Abby opened her eyes and looked at Grandma. "Was Mary scared?" she asked.

Grandma's expression grew tender. "She might have been," she said. "But she also trusted God. She knew that this baby was part of His plan, and she believed that He would take care of them."

IN ABBY'S MIND, THE scene unfolded. She saw Mary resting on a bed of hay, her breaths coming in quick, steady rhythms. Joseph knelt beside her, his hands steady but his face etched with concern. The stable was dimly lit by a single lantern, its glow casting warm shadows on the wooden walls.

And then, after hours of waiting, the cry of a newborn pierced the stillness.

"Jesus was born that night," Grandma said, her voice filled with wonder. "The Savior of the world, born in the humblest of places. Mary wrapped Him in swaddling clothes and laid Him in a manger—a feeding trough filled with hay."

The children sat in awed silence, the weight of the moment settling over them. Abby imagined the tiny baby, His face soft and peaceful, lying in the manger. She could almost hear the rustle of the animals moving nearby, their warm breath creating a quiet hush in the stable.

"Why wasn't Jesus born in a palace?" Ben asked suddenly, his brow furrowed. "He's the King of Kings, right?"

Grandma smiled, her eyes twinkling. "That's a wonderful question, Ben. Jesus wasn't born in a palace because He came to show us that God's love is for everyone—not just for kings and rulers, but for shepherds, fishermen, and even children like you. His humble birth reminds us that no one is too small or unimportant for God's love."

GRANDMA TURNED THE page of the Bible, her voice steady. "Now, imagine the shepherds on the hills outside Bethlehem. They were keeping watch over their flocks when suddenly, an angel appeared, shining brightly in the night. The angel said, 'Fear not: for, behold, I bring you good tidings of great joy, which shall be to all people. For unto you is born this day in the city of David a Saviour, which is Christ the Lord.'"

The children gasped, their faces lighting up. Abby imagined the shepherds staring in amazement as the angel spoke, their hearts racing with both fear and joy.

"The angel told the shepherds where to find Jesus," Grandma continued. "And they hurried to the stable, where they found Mary and Joseph, and the baby lying in the manger. They were the first to hear the good news and to see the Savior of the world."

ABBY COULDN'T HELP but smile, her heart full. She pictured the shepherds kneeling by the manger, their faces glowing with awe as they gazed at the tiny baby. The scene felt so real, so alive, as if she could step into it and be there herself.

"What do you think the shepherds felt when they saw Jesus?" Grandma asked, her gaze sweeping over the children.

"Happy," Abby said softly. "And amazed. Like they couldn't believe they were really seeing Him."

"That's right," Grandma said, her smile widening. "And that's how we should feel every time we think about Jesus' birth. It's a reminder of how much God loves us—that He sent His Son into the world to be our Savior."

AS THE FIRE BURNED low and the room grew quieter, Grandma closed the Bible and looked at the children. "The story of Jesus' birth isn't just something that happened a long time ago," she said. "It's a story for us today. It reminds us to keep our hearts open, to share God's love with others, and to always remember that Jesus came for all of us."

The children nodded, their faces thoughtful. Abby felt a warmth in her chest, a deep sense of joy that stayed with her as the evening went on.

LATER THAT NIGHT, AS Abby lay in bed, she whispered a quiet prayer. "Thank You, Jesus, for coming to the world, even in a little stable. Help me to always remember how much You love us."

And as she drifted off to sleep, she felt a sense of peace, knowing that the story of Jesus' birth was not just a story—it was the greatest gift of all.

Day 9 - The Angels Announce the Good News

The living room was alive with warmth and light as Ben sat cross-legged on the carpet, a mug of hot cocoa in his hands. The Christmas tree sparkled nearby, its ornaments reflecting the soft glow of the fireplace. Abby sat beside him, twirling a candy cane in her fingers, while their dad leaned back in the armchair, holding an open Bible.

"Can we hear the story about the angels and the shepherds?" Ben asked, his eyes bright with excitement. "That's my favorite part of Christmas."

Dad smiled, setting his Bible on his lap. "It's one of my favorite parts, too. The angels announcing Jesus' birth is a story full of joy, wonder, and hope. Are you ready to hear it?"

Ben nodded eagerly, scooting closer. Abby leaned forward, just as curious, even though she'd heard the story many times before.

DAD BEGAN, HIS VOICE warm and steady. "On the night Jesus was born, the town of Bethlehem was quiet. But just outside the town, shepherds were watching over their flocks. It was an ordinary night for them, just like so many others."

Ben closed his eyes, imagining the scene. In his mind, he saw the shepherds sitting around a crackling fire on a grassy hillside. The stars twinkled above them, and their sheep rested nearby, the soft bleating of lambs mixing with the occasional rustle of the wind through the grass.

Dad's voice drew Ben back. "Suddenly, something incredible happened. The sky lit up with a bright, glorious light, and an angel appeared before them."

BEN COULD ALMOST SEE it now—the shepherds shielding their eyes as the angel appeared, glowing with a radiance brighter than anything they had ever seen. The hills were bathed in a warm, golden light, and the peaceful night was filled with something new and powerful: the presence of God.

"The shepherds were terrified," Dad continued, "but the angel spoke to them, saying, 'Fear not: for, behold, I bring you good tidings of great joy, which shall be to all people.'"

"What does 'good tidings' mean?" Abby asked, interrupting.

"It means good news," Dad explained. "The angel was telling the shepherds about something amazing—something that would change the world forever."

Ben's heart raced as Dad went on. "The angel said, 'For unto you is born this day in the city of David a Saviour, which is Christ the Lord.' And then the angel gave them a sign: they would find the baby wrapped in swaddling clothes, lying in a manger."

BEN OPENED HIS EYES, trying to picture the shepherds' faces as they listened. Did they feel as awestruck as he did, sitting here now? He imagined the shepherds glancing at one another, their fear fading and being replaced by a growing sense of wonder. Could it really be true? The long-awaited Savior, born on this very night?

"But that wasn't all," Dad said, his voice rising slightly. "Suddenly, the sky was filled with even more angels—a multitude of the heavenly host. They praised God, saying, 'Glory to God in the highest, and on earth peace, good will toward men.'"

Ben's breath caught as he imagined it. The quiet hillside transformed into a scene of unimaginable glory, the sky filled with shimmering angels singing in perfect harmony. Their voices were like a thousand instruments, powerful yet gentle, lifting up a song that filled the world with hope and joy.

"What do you think the shepherds did next?" Dad asked, looking at Ben and Abby.

"They ran to see Jesus!" Ben exclaimed, his voice filled with excitement.

"That's exactly right," Dad said, smiling. "As soon as the angels left and the sky grew dark again, the shepherds hurried into Bethlehem. They wanted to see for themselves the incredible thing God had done."

BEN CLOSED HIS EYES again, letting the story play out in his mind. He saw the shepherds leaving their flocks behind, their footsteps quick and purposeful as they made their way into the town. The streets of Bethlehem were still crowded, but the shepherds didn't stop to rest or ask questions. They followed the angel's words, their hearts filled with anticipation.

Finally, they reached the stable. It was small and humble, just as the angel had said. Inside, a soft light glowed, and the shepherds saw Mary and Joseph, with a tiny baby lying in a manger.

Ben imagined the shepherds kneeling beside the manger, their faces lit with awe. This was Him—the Savior, the Messiah, the One they had waited for. The baby didn't look like a king, lying there wrapped in simple cloths, but there was something about Him that made their hearts swell with joy.

"The shepherds were the first to see Jesus," Dad said, his voice soft. "And after they saw Him, they couldn't keep the news to themselves. They went out and told everyone what the angel had said and what they had seen. They shared the good news, and everyone who heard it was amazed."

"DO YOU THINK THEY WERE scared to tell people?" Abby asked, tilting her head.

"Maybe at first," Dad said thoughtfully. "But their joy was stronger than their fear. When you experience something as wonderful as meeting Jesus, it's hard to keep it to yourself. The shepherds couldn't wait to share the news."

Ben grinned, imagining himself running through the streets of Bethlehem, shouting, "The Savior is here! He's born!"

LATER THAT EVENING, after Dad had finished reading the story and they'd said goodnight, Ben lay in bed, staring up at the ceiling. His mind was still full of the angel's announcement and the shepherds' journey to the stable. What would it have been like to hear the heavenly host singing? To see the Savior, lying in a manger?

Ben whispered into the quiet darkness, "Jesus, thank You for coming to earth. Thank You for being our Savior. Help me to share Your good news, just like the shepherds did."

As he drifted off to sleep, Ben imagined the angels' song echoing through the hills, filling the world with a joy that would never end.

Day 10 - The Shepherds Visit Jesus

The classroom buzzed with quiet excitement as Daniel stood near the front, holding a small book in his hands. It was his turn to share something special during Sunday school, and he had chosen one of his favorite stories from the Bible: the shepherds visiting Jesus. A large nativity scene was set up on a table beside him, complete with tiny figurines of Mary, Joseph, baby Jesus, and a group of shepherds, their features carved with care and detail.

Daniel took a deep breath, looking out at the faces of his classmates. They were watching him expectantly, waiting for the story to begin.

"Today, I want to tell you about the shepherds," he said, his voice steady but a little nervous. "Their journey to see Jesus shows us that God welcomes everyone, no matter who they are or where they come from."

Miss Clara, their teacher, gave him an encouraging nod. "Go ahead, Daniel," she said warmly. "We're excited to hear your story."

DANIEL TOOK ANOTHER deep breath and began. "The shepherds were out in the fields at night, taking care of their sheep. It was probably dark and quiet, except for the sounds of the sheep bleating and the wind moving through the grass."

He paused, his imagination filling in the scene. "They were just ordinary people, doing their job. Nobody really paid much attention to shepherds back then. They weren't important or rich, and they didn't have fancy clothes or big houses. But that night, something amazing happened."

Daniel's voice grew more confident as he went on. "Suddenly, an angel appeared to them, and the glory of God lit up the sky. The shepherds were so scared! But the angel told them not to be afraid because he had good news—news that would bring joy to everyone. The Savior, Christ the Lord, had been born in Bethlehem."

MISS CLARA STEPPED in briefly, her tone gentle. "What do you think the shepherds felt when they heard that news, class? Surprised? Excited?"

The children nodded, their faces lit with wonder.

Daniel smiled. "I think they were all those things. The angel told them they would find the baby wrapped in swaddling clothes and lying in a manger. And then—" Daniel's voice rose with excitement—"the sky filled with more angels! A whole host of them, singing and praising God, saying, 'Glory to God in the highest, and on earth peace, good will toward men.'"

Daniel's classmates gasped softly, their eyes wide as they imagined the sky filled with brilliant, singing angels.

DANIEL CONTINUED, NOW fully engrossed in the story. "When the angels went back to heaven, the shepherds didn't wait. They said, 'Let's go to Bethlehem and see what the Lord has told us.' They left their sheep and hurried into town."

He picked up one of the shepherd figurines from the nativity scene and held it up for everyone to see. "These guys didn't stop to change their clothes or clean up. They went just as they were, excited to meet the Savior."

IN DANIEL'S MIND, HE could see the shepherds making their way through the dark streets of Bethlehem. They were still catching their breath from the angels' visit, their hearts racing with both joy and nervousness. They didn't know exactly where to look, but they trusted the angel's words. Step by step, they searched until finally, they came to a small stable at the edge of town.

Daniel set the figurine down beside the manger in the nativity scene. "When they got there," he said, his voice softening, "they found Mary and Joseph, just like the angel said. And there, lying in a manger, was baby Jesus."

THE ROOM WAS QUIET as Daniel paused, letting the weight of the moment sink in. "The shepherds were the first people to see Jesus—the Son of God. They didn't have fancy gifts like the wise men would bring later. They just came as they were, and God welcomed them."

MISS CLARA SMILED, stepping forward again. "Why do you think God chose the shepherds to hear the good news first?" she asked the class.

One of the younger boys raised his hand. "Maybe because they didn't have anything to prove. They just believed."

"That's a great answer," Miss Clara said. "God didn't send the angels to kings or priests. He chose shepherds—ordinary, humble people—to show that His love is for everyone."

Daniel nodded, picking up where he left off. "After the shepherds saw Jesus, they couldn't keep it to themselves. They went out and told everyone they could find. They said, 'The Savior is here!' And people were amazed."

IN HIS MIND, DANIEL pictured the shepherds running through the streets, their faces glowing with joy. They knocked on doors, stopped strangers in the market, and shared the incredible news with anyone who would listen. "This wasn't just for them," Daniel said, his voice filled with conviction. "It was for everyone."

HE LOOKED BACK AT HIS classmates, his eyes bright. "What I love about this story is that it shows us how much God loves us. The shepherds weren't rich or important, but they were the first to hear the good news. That means it doesn't matter where we come from or what we have—God welcomes us just as we are."

MISS CLARA CLAPPED her hands softly. "Thank you, Daniel. That was a beautiful way to share the story."

The class nodded in agreement, their faces thoughtful. Abby raised her hand. "I think it's cool that the shepherds didn't bring gifts. It shows that God doesn't want things from us—He just wants us to come to Him."

"Exactly," Miss Clara said, her smile widening. "God wants our hearts, our love, and our trust. That's the greatest gift we can give Him."

THAT EVENING, AS DANIEL sat by the window in his room, he thought about the shepherds again. He pictured them standing in the stable, gazing at baby Jesus with awe and wonder. They didn't have riches or treasures to offer, but they gave something even more precious: their belief, their joy, and their willingness to share the good news.

Daniel whispered a quiet prayer. "Thank You, God, for welcoming everyone—even people like the shepherds, and people like me. Help me to always remember that Your love is for everyone, no matter what."

As he lay down to sleep, the image of the shepherds stayed with him, a reminder of the simple, powerful truth of that first Christmas: God's love knows no limits, and His arms are open to all.

Day 11 - The Heavenly Choir

The classroom hummed with anticipation as Miss Clara adjusted the sparkly wings on Chloe's back. The children had gathered for their annual Christmas play rehearsal, and today was the moment Chloe had been waiting for: her turn to pretend to be an angel, leading the heavenly choir.

"You're going to do great, Chloe," Miss Clara said, her eyes warm and encouraging. "Just remember to smile and speak loudly. This is one of the most important parts of the story."

Chloe nodded, her cheeks flushed with excitement. She had been practicing her lines all week, standing in front of her bedroom mirror and imagining the hills of Bethlehem glowing with angelic light. Now, she was ready to bring the moment to life.

THE REHEARSAL BEGAN, the makeshift stage buzzing with activity. The shepherds—played by a group of wiggly second-graders—sat around a pretend campfire, their "sheep" scattered around them in the form of stuffed animals. Chloe waited behind the curtain, her wings brushing against the fabric as she rehearsed her lines silently.

Miss Clara's voice narrated the scene. "That night, the shepherds were in the fields, keeping watch over their flocks. It was an ordinary evening, quiet and still."

On cue, Chloe stepped onto the stage, her white robe glimmering under the soft yellow lights. The shepherds gasped dramatically, shielding their eyes with their hands.

"And suddenly," Miss Clara continued, "an angel of the Lord appeared to them, and the glory of the Lord shone around them."

Chloe raised her arms, her voice steady and clear as she spoke. "Fear not! For behold, I bring you good tidings of great joy, which shall be to all people. For unto you is born this day in the city of David a Savior, which is Christ the Lord."

The shepherds looked at one another, their expressions a mix of awe and confusion. Then, at Miss Clara's signal, the rest of the "angels" joined Chloe on stage, forming a sparkling choir behind her.

"And suddenly," Miss Clara narrated, her voice lifting with excitement, "there was with the angel a multitude of the heavenly host, praising God and saying..."

Chloe took a deep breath, her heart swelling with the wonder of the moment. Together with the other children, she sang out, "Glory to God in the highest, and on earth peace, good will toward men."

WHEN THE SONG ENDED, the room erupted in applause. Miss Clara clapped her hands, her face glowing with pride. "Beautiful, everyone! That was absolutely beautiful."

Chloe's cheeks hurt from smiling so much as she stepped down from the stage. She joined the other children on the rug, still wearing her angel wings. Her mind was filled with the image of the shepherds on the hillside, their faces bathed in heavenly light as the angels filled the night sky with song.

LATER, DURING SNACK time, the children gathered around Miss Clara, their excitement still buzzing. "Miss Clara," Chloe said, her voice thoughtful, "do you think the angels sounded like us when they sang?"

Miss Clara smiled, setting down the plate of cookies she had been arranging. "I think the angels' song must have been the most beautiful sound anyone had ever heard," she said. "But I also think that when we sing to praise God, it's just as beautiful to Him."

The children looked at her curiously. "Even if we're not good at singing?" one of the younger boys asked, his face scrunched with doubt.

Miss Clara knelt down, her kind eyes meeting his. "Even if we're not perfect singers," she said. "God doesn't care about how we sound—He cares about what's in our hearts. When we praise Him, we're joining in the same song the angels sang that night, giving glory to God."

CHLOE TILTED HER HEAD, her mind turning over the thought. "So, when we sing at church or at home, it's like we're part of the heavenly choir?"

Miss Clara nodded. "Exactly, Chloe. Every time we sing to God, whether it's in a big group or all by ourselves, we're adding our voices to the song of praise that's been going on since that first Christmas night."

THAT EVENING, AFTER rehearsal ended and the children returned home, Chloe found herself humming the angel's song as she helped her mom set the table for dinner. The words felt different now—not just something to memorize for the play, but something alive and powerful. "Glory to God in the highest," she whispered under her breath, imagining the starry sky above Bethlehem and the angels filling it with light.

Her mom noticed her humming and smiled. "You seem happy, Chloe. What's on your mind?"

Chloe hesitated, then said, "We talked about how singing praises to God is like joining the angels' song. I think it's really cool that we get to do that."

Her mom nodded, her expression thoughtful. "It is cool. And it's not just singing, Chloe. We can praise God in lots of ways—through our words, our prayers, even how we treat other people. Everything we do can be a way of saying, 'Glory to God.'"

THAT NIGHT, CHLOE LAY in bed, staring up at the glow-in-the-dark stars on her ceiling. She thought about the angels, their voices echoing across the hills as they celebrated Jesus' birth. She imagined herself standing among them, her small voice joining their mighty chorus. It made her feel small in a good way—like she was part of something much bigger than herself.

Before she fell asleep, she whispered a quiet prayer. "Thank You, God, for sending Jesus to us. And thank You for letting us be part of Your song. Help me to praise You in everything I do."

THE NEXT DAY AT REHEARSAL, Chloe wore her angel wings with pride, not because they made her look special, but because they reminded her of her new role in the heavenly choir. When it was time to sing, she raised her voice confidently, knowing that her song mattered—not just to her classmates or Miss Clara, but to God.

Day 12 - The Stable: A Humble Beginning

The kitchen was warm and cozy, filled with the rich aroma of freshly baked cookies. Abby sat at the large wooden table with her younger brother, Ben, and their cousins, Jonah and Mia. Their mom bustled about, transferring cookies onto a cooling rack while the children sipped hot cocoa from brightly colored mugs. A soft snowfall outside the window added to the magic of the evening, the flakes swirling in the golden glow of the porch light.

"Mom," Abby began, her eyes thoughtful as she traced a finger along the rim of her mug, "why was Jesus born in a stable? It doesn't seem like the kind of place for a king."

Her mom paused, setting down the tray of cookies. She turned to Abby with a warm smile, her hands resting on her hips. "That's a very good question, sweetheart. Why don't we talk about it while the cookies cool?"

The children perked up at the prospect of a story, their cocoa forgotten for the moment. Abby's mom pulled out a chair and sat down at the table, her eyes sparkling with the kind of wisdom that always seemed to calm and inspire at the same time.

"Let's start by remembering what happened that night," she said, her voice soft but full of wonder. "Mary and Joseph had traveled all the way to Bethlehem because of the census. By the time they arrived, the town was packed. People had come from all over, and every inn was full."

ABBY IMAGINED THE CROWDED streets, the sounds of donkeys braying and carts rumbling over the cobblestones. She pictured Mary and Joseph, weary from their journey, searching for a place to stay as the night grew darker.

"The Bible tells us there was no room for them in the inn," her mom continued. "But one kind innkeeper offered them shelter in a stable—a simple place meant for animals, not for people."

Ben wrinkled his nose. "A stable? Like, with cows and sheep and stuff? That doesn't sound very nice."

"It wasn't," Abby's mom agreed. "It was probably dirty and smelled like hay and animals. It wasn't the kind of place you'd expect a king to be born."

JONAH LEANED FORWARD, his brow furrowed. "Then why would God let His Son be born there? Shouldn't Jesus have been born in a palace or something fancy?"

Abby's mom nodded, her expression thoughtful. "You're right, Jonah. Jesus is the King of Kings, and He could have been born in the grandest palace, surrounded by wealth and power. But God chose for His Son to come into the world in a humble stable. Do you know why?"

The children shook their heads, their curiosity piqued.

"Because God wanted to show us that His love isn't just for the rich or the powerful," she said. "It's for everyone. By being born in a stable, Jesus showed that He came for the ordinary and the overlooked—for shepherds, farmers, and people like you and me."

MIA'S EYES WIDENED. "So, Jesus was showing us that it doesn't matter how fancy or important we are?"

"Exactly," her mom said, her smile widening. "Jesus' birth in a stable teaches us the value of humility. He didn't come to show off or demand special treatment. He came to serve, to love, and to teach us how to do the same."

AS HER MOM SPOKE, ABBY'S mind filled with the scene of the stable. She imagined the soft glow of a lantern illuminating the rough wooden walls, the hay piled high in the corners, and the gentle sounds of animals shifting in their stalls. In the midst of it all, she pictured Mary cradling baby Jesus, her face radiant with joy despite the humble surroundings.

"Think about it," her mom said, pulling Abby from her thoughts. "The stable wasn't perfect, but it was peaceful. It was quiet. It was a place where the shepherds could come and kneel before Jesus without feeling out of place. God chose the stable for a reason."

BEN TILTED HIS HEAD, his expression thoughtful. "So, being humble means not trying to be better than everyone else?"

"That's part of it," Abby's mom said. "Being humble means putting others before yourself, not thinking you're more important than anyone else, and being willing to serve, even when it's not easy. Jesus showed us what humility looks like from the very beginning—by being born in a stable."

THE CHILDREN SAT QUIETLY for a moment, letting the lesson sink in. Abby thought about her own life—about the times she had insisted on being first in line, or when she'd bragged about getting a higher grade than her classmates. Was that the kind of attitude Jesus wanted her to have?

HER MOM STOOD AND WALKED over to the nativity set on the mantle. She picked up the tiny figure of baby Jesus and held it in her hands. "When we look at this nativity, we see a beautiful scene. But it's also a reminder that God's love often shows up in the simplest, humblest ways. Jesus came into the world quietly, without fanfare, to show us that greatness doesn't come from power or riches—it comes from love, kindness, and humility."

THAT NIGHT, AS ABBY lay in bed, she thought about the stable and what it meant. She thought about Jesus, the Son of God, lying in a manger surrounded by hay and animals. It was so different from how she had always imagined a king, but somehow, it felt even more special.

"Jesus," she whispered into the darkness, "thank You for being born in a stable and showing us how to be humble. Help me to be more like You."

THE NEXT DAY, ABBY carried the lesson with her. At school, when her friend needed help finishing an art project, Abby stayed late to lend a hand instead of rushing home to watch her favorite show. When Ben accidentally spilled his juice at lunch, she didn't scold him—instead, she grabbed a towel and helped clean it up.

With each small act of kindness, Abby felt a warmth in her heart, as if the spirit of the stable was still with her. And as Christmas drew closer, she realized that the story of Jesus' humble beginning wasn't just something to hear and admire—it was something to live.

Day 13 - The Star of Bethlehem

The living room was bathed in soft golden light, the Christmas tree standing proudly in the corner with its twinkling ornaments and strands of sparkling tinsel. Abby, Ben, and their cousins Jonah and Mia gathered on the floor near the fireplace, their faces glowing with curiosity. Above the mantle, a glittering star ornament hung at the center of the nativity scene, catching the firelight.

Grandpa James, with his silver hair and warm smile, sat in his armchair, a thick Bible resting on his lap. Tonight, he was going to tell them a story about the star of Bethlehem—the mysterious light that had guided the wise men to find baby Jesus.

"All right, kids," Grandpa began, his deep voice filling the room. "Have you ever wondered why we put a star on top of the Christmas tree?"

"It's because of the star of Bethlehem, right?" Jonah asked, leaning forward.

"That's right," Grandpa said with a nod. "But do you know the whole story? The star wasn't just a decoration in the sky—it was a sign, a guide, and a promise fulfilled. Let me tell you about it."

The children grew quiet, their eyes fixed on Grandpa as he opened his Bible to the book of Matthew.

"AFTER JESUS WAS BORN in Bethlehem," Grandpa read, "wise men from the east came to Jerusalem, saying, 'Where is he that is born King of the Jews? For we have seen his star in the east, and are come to worship him.'"

Abby tilted her head, her brow furrowed. "Who were the wise men, Grandpa?"

"They were scholars," Grandpa explained, "people who studied the stars and the ancient writings of different cultures. They lived far away, in a place where they might not have even known about the God of Israel. But they saw something extraordinary in the sky—a star unlike any other. They believed it was a sign of a great king's birth."

IN THE CHILDREN'S IMAGINATIONS, the story unfolded. They pictured the wise men—wrapped in long robes, their faces lined with wisdom—standing on a desert hill beneath a dark, starry sky. One of them pointed upward, his voice filled with awe as he spoke of the brilliant star that had appeared, shining brighter than all the others.

Grandpa continued, his voice carrying a tone of reverence. "The wise men didn't know exactly where the star would lead them, but they trusted that it was guiding them to someone important. So, they packed their treasures—gold, frankincense, and myrrh—and began a long journey westward."

Ben's eyes widened. "How far did they have to go?"

"Very far," Grandpa said. "It might have taken them weeks, or even months. They traveled through deserts and mountains, trusting the star to show them the way. And eventually, it brought them to Jerusalem."

THE CHILDREN IMAGINED the bustling streets of Jerusalem, filled with merchants, travelers, and Roman soldiers. The wise men, weary from their journey but driven by determination, asked everyone they met: "Where is the newborn king? We've seen His star."

"When King Herod heard about the wise men," Grandpa went on, "he was troubled. He called his priests and scribes and asked them where the Messiah was supposed to be born."

"In Bethlehem," Mia said confidently, remembering what she'd learned in Sunday school.

"That's right," Grandpa said with a smile. "The scriptures had foretold it long ago: 'And thou Bethlehem, in the land of Judah, art not the least among the princes of Judah: for out of thee shall come a Governor, that shall rule my people Israel.' So Herod told the wise men to go to Bethlehem and search for the child. He said, 'When you find Him, let me know so I can worship Him too.'"

"But he didn't really want to worship Jesus, did he?" Abby asked, her face serious.

Grandpa shook his head. "No, Herod was afraid of losing his throne. He wanted to stop Jesus from becoming king. But God's plans can't be stopped."

THE CHILDREN LISTENED, spellbound, as Grandpa described the next part of the journey. "The wise men followed the star to Bethlehem, and it came to rest over the place where Jesus was. When they saw the star, they rejoiced with exceeding great joy."

In their minds, they pictured the wise men standing before a small, humble house. The star above them bathed everything in a soft, heavenly glow. Inside, Mary held baby Jesus, her face serene and radiant.

"The wise men went inside," Grandpa said, his voice softening, "and they knelt down to worship Him. They opened their treasures and offered Him gifts—gold for a king, frankincense for a priest, and myrrh, which symbolized sacrifice. Even though they were strangers from a faraway land, they recognized that this child was someone extraordinary. He was the Savior of the world."

GRANDPA CLOSED THE Bible gently, looking at the children with a thoughtful expression. "The star of Bethlehem wasn't just a light in the sky," he said. "It was God's way of leading the wise men to Jesus. And do you know what? God still leads us to Jesus today."

The children exchanged curious glances. "How?" Ben asked.

"Not with a star, but in other ways," Grandpa explained. "Sometimes He uses the Bible, which is like a map that shows us the way to Jesus. Sometimes He uses people—like pastors, teachers, or even friends—who point us toward Him. And sometimes, He speaks to our hearts, giving us a desire to know Him."

ABBY LOOKED AT THE star ornament above the nativity scene, its golden points catching the firelight. "So, the star is like a reminder," she said slowly. "It reminds us that God is always leading us."

"Exactly," Grandpa said, his smile widening. "The wise men didn't find Jesus by accident. They found Him because they were searching, and God guided them every step of the way. And if we're searching for Jesus, God will guide us, too."

THAT NIGHT, AS ABBY lay in bed, she thought about the wise men and their journey. She thought about how much they must have trusted the star, even when the road was long and uncertain. Could she trust God like that? Could she follow where He led, even when she didn't know exactly where she was going?

Before closing her eyes, she whispered a quiet prayer. "Thank You, God, for guiding the wise men to Jesus. Please guide me, too. Help me to follow You, just like they followed the star."

THE NEXT DAY, AS ABBY and Ben played outside in the snow, they paused to look up at the sky. It was bright and clear, and though the stars wouldn't appear until nightfall, Abby felt a sense of peace as she remembered the story. The star of Bethlehem wasn't just a part of history—it was a promise that God still leads His people, lighting the way to Jesus for anyone willing to follow.

And that, she thought, was the best kind of light there could ever be.

Day 14 - The Wise Men's Journey

The snow had stopped falling outside, leaving a blanket of white glistening under the streetlights. Inside the living room, the warmth of the fireplace filled the air, and Ben sat cross-legged on the rug, staring at the nativity scene on the mantle. His eyes were drawn to the small figurines of the wise men, each holding a tiny gift, their camels resting beside them. He had always been fascinated by their story—how they traveled so far, following nothing but a star, all to find baby Jesus.

"Mom," Ben said, turning toward her as she folded laundry on the couch. "How did the wise men know where to go? I mean, a star is just a star, right? What if they got lost?"

His mom smiled, setting down a pile of folded towels. She walked over to sit beside him, her gaze resting on the nativity. "That's a great question, Ben. The wise men didn't have GPS or maps like we do today. But they were guided by something even better—faith. They trusted that the star was leading them to someone very special."

BEN TILTED HIS HEAD, thinking about her words. "But why did they go so far? Couldn't they have just waited for Jesus to come to them?"

"That's another great question," his mom said, her voice soft and thoughtful. "The wise men's journey shows us something important: when we know Jesus is worth finding, we're willing to go the extra mile—even when it's hard."

She leaned forward, her eyes sparkling with excitement. "Would you like to hear the whole story? It's one of my favorites."

Ben nodded eagerly, leaning back against the couch as his mom began.

"AFTER JESUS WAS BORN in Bethlehem," she started, "a group of wise men—sometimes called magi—saw a special star in the sky. They believed this star was a sign that a great king had been born, so they decided to follow it. They didn't know exactly where it would lead, but they were determined to find Him."

Ben closed his eyes, letting his imagination take over. He pictured the wise men standing on a desert hill, their robes rippling in the cool evening breeze. Above them, the night sky stretched wide and endless, stars twinkling like tiny diamonds. But one star outshone them all—a brilliant light that seemed to beckon them forward.

"THEY CAME FROM THE east," his mom continued, "probably from a place far, far away. The journey wasn't easy. They had to travel through deserts, across mountains, and through busy towns, all while keeping their eyes on the star."

"How long did it take them?" Ben asked, his voice filled with awe.

"Maybe months, maybe longer," his mom said. "They were determined to find Jesus, no matter how long it took."

IN BEN'S MIND, THE journey came alive. He saw the wise men riding on camels, their silhouettes moving against the golden sands of the desert. The sun beat down on them during the day, and the cold wind chilled them at night, but still, they pressed on, the star their only guide. They camped under the open sky, sharing quiet conversations around the fire, their hearts full of hope and wonder.

"What kept them going?" Ben asked, opening his eyes to look at his mom. "Didn't they get tired or want to give up?"

"I'm sure they got tired," his mom said with a smile. "But they kept going because they knew the journey was worth it. They were searching for the Savior, the King of Kings. That kind of hope can give you strength, even when things get hard."

SHE CONTINUED THE STORY, her voice steady and calm. "Eventually, the wise men arrived in Jerusalem, the capital city. They went to King Herod and asked, 'Where is He who has been born King of the Jews? We have seen His star in the east and have come to worship Him.'"

Ben frowned. "Why didn't they just go straight to Jesus?"

"Well," his mom explained, "they thought a king would be born in a palace, so they went to the place where kings lived. But Herod wasn't happy about their question. He was jealous and didn't want anyone to take his throne."

Ben's brow furrowed. "So what did Herod do?"

"He told the wise men to go to Bethlehem and find the child, pretending he wanted to worship Him too," she said. "But really, Herod had other plans. The wise men didn't know that yet, though. They left Jerusalem and followed the star again."

IN BEN'S MIND, THE story unfolded like a vivid dream. He saw the wise men leaving the city gates, the star glowing brighter as it guided them along winding roads and quiet fields. Then, at last, the star stopped, its light resting over a small, humble house in Bethlehem.

"When they saw the star stop, they rejoiced with exceeding great joy," his mom said, her voice lifting with excitement. "They had finally found Him."

BEN COULD SEE IT ALL so clearly now—the wise men stepping into the quiet house, their eyes widening as they saw Mary holding baby Jesus. The room was simple, with rough wooden beams and a dirt floor, but to the wise men, it was more glorious than any palace. They knelt before the child, their hearts full of awe.

"They brought Him gifts," his mom said. "Gold, because Jesus is the King of Kings. Frankincense, because He is our High Priest. And myrrh, because He would one day give His life for us."

BEN SAT IN SILENCE, his heart swelling as he imagined the wise men laying their treasures at Jesus' feet. They had traveled so far, through so many challenges, and now they were here, face-to-face with the Savior. It must have been the most incredible moment of their lives.

"What happened after that?" Ben asked quietly.

"They were warned in a dream not to go back to Herod," his mom said. "So they returned to their own country another way, still carrying the joy of knowing they had met Jesus."

FOR A LONG MOMENT, Ben stared at the wise men in the nativity scene, their tiny faces frozen in expressions of reverence. "I think the wise men were really brave," he said finally. "They didn't know where the star would take them, but they trusted it anyway."

His mom nodded. "That's right, Ben. The wise men teach us an important lesson: when we truly want to find Jesus, we have to be willing to follow, even when it's hard or uncertain. And just like the star guided the wise men, God will guide us if we're looking for Him."

THAT NIGHT, AS BEN lay in bed, he thought about the wise men and their incredible journey. He thought about their determination, their courage, and their faith. He wondered if he would have the same strength to keep going, even when the road was long and difficult.

Closing his eyes, he whispered a quiet prayer. "Jesus, help me to be like the wise men. Help me to follow You, no matter where it takes me."

As he drifted off to sleep, he imagined himself on a journey of his own, following a brilliant star across a wide, open sky. And in his heart, he knew the destination was worth every step.

Day 15 - The Gifts for the King

The scent of cinnamon and pine filled the living room as Chloe sat cross-legged on the carpet, gazing at the nativity scene on the coffee table. Her mom had just finished reading the story of the wise men bringing their gifts to baby Jesus, and now Chloe's mind was alive with questions. She leaned forward, her eyes fixed on the tiny figures of the three wise men. Each one held a small treasure—a gleaming chest of gold, a delicate jar of frankincense, and a slender flask of myrrh.

"Mom," Chloe asked, her voice thoughtful, "why did they bring those gifts? I mean, why not toys or blankets for the baby?"

Her mom, seated nearby with a mug of tea in her hands, smiled at the question. "Those gifts were very special, Chloe," she said. "They weren't just practical—they were meaningful. Each one said something important about who Jesus is."

Chloe tilted her head, trying to imagine what it must have been like to kneel before baby Jesus and offer such treasures. "What do they mean?" she asked.

"Well," her mom began, setting her tea aside, "gold was a gift for a king. It showed that Jesus is the King of Kings. Frankincense was used in worship, like incense in the temple. It reminded everyone that Jesus is God. And myrrh—" she paused, her voice softening—"myrrh was used to prepare bodies for burial. It pointed to the sacrifice Jesus would one day make for us."

CHLOE SAT BACK, LETTING the words sink in. She closed her eyes and imagined the scene, the story unfolding in her mind.

The room was simple, its walls made of rough stone, illuminated by the soft glow of an oil lamp. Mary sat on a low stool, cradling baby Jesus in her arms, her face serene and radiant. Joseph stood nearby, his protective gaze resting on them both.

The door creaked open, and three men entered, their robes rich and flowing, their expressions a mixture of awe and reverence. Chloe could almost hear the gentle shuffle of their sandals on the floor as they approached the tiny family.

"We have traveled far," one of them said, his voice deep and steady. "We followed the star, seeking the One who is born King of the Jews."

The first wise man stepped forward and knelt, holding out a chest filled with shining gold. The coins caught the light, their brilliance reflecting the majesty of the moment. Chloe imagined the man's thoughts as he offered his gift: This is for the King, a treasure worthy of His greatness.

The second wise man knelt next, presenting a jar of frankincense. A soft, fragrant aroma filled the room as he opened it, the scent rising like a prayer to heaven. In Chloe's mind, she could almost hear the man's whisper: This is for the Son of God, a gift of worship and devotion.

Then the third wise man approached, his movements slower, more deliberate. He held a flask of myrrh, its purpose somber and significant. He placed it gently before Mary, his voice low as he said, "This is for the Savior, the One who will give His life for the world."

CHLOE OPENED HER EYES, her heart full as she returned to the present. The scene she had imagined felt so real, so alive, and now she saw the gifts in a new light.

"Mom," she said slowly, "the wise men gave Jesus such special gifts. But what can we give Him? We don't have gold or frankincense or myrrh."

Her mom's smile widened, and she reached out to touch Chloe's shoulder. "That's a beautiful question, Chloe. The wise men brought treasures because they wanted to honor Jesus. But what Jesus wants most from us is something much simpler."

"What?" Chloe asked, her curiosity piqued.

"Our hearts," her mom said gently. "Jesus wants our love, our trust, and our devotion. When we choose to follow Him, to be kind, to share, to forgive, we're giving Him a gift that's more precious than gold."

CHLOE THOUGHT ABOUT this, her mind swirling with possibilities. She imagined herself standing before Jesus, holding out her hands. What could she give Him? What would make Him smile?

That evening, as she helped her mom clear the dinner table, Chloe found herself thinking about small ways to show love. When Ben spilled his milk, she grabbed a towel without complaining. When her dad asked for help putting away the Christmas decorations, she said yes, even though she'd rather be drawing.

"Mom," she said later that night as they sat together by the fire, "do you think doing little things like helping and sharing can really be a gift for Jesus?"

Her mom nodded, her eyes warm with pride. "Absolutely, Chloe. Every time you show kindness or love, you're reflecting His light. And that's a gift He treasures more than anything."

BEFORE BED, CHLOE KNELT beside her window, looking out at the clear, starry sky. She thought about the wise men again—their long journey, their precious gifts, and their hearts full of worship. She thought about what her mom had said, and slowly, she folded her hands and whispered a prayer.

"Jesus, I don't have gold or frankincense or myrrh. But I want to give You my heart. Help me to follow You, to love You, and to show Your love to others."

As she climbed into bed, she felt a warmth in her chest, as if Jesus Himself had heard her prayer and smiled. And as she drifted off to sleep, she dreamed of stars and gifts and the greatest King the world had ever known.

THE NEXT MORNING, CHLOE woke up with a sense of purpose. She decided to start small, just like her mom had said. She made a card for her neighbor, Mrs. Brown, who had been feeling lonely. She let Ben pick what they watched on TV, even though it wasn't her favorite show. And when her mom asked if she wanted to help bake cookies for the food bank, Chloe said yes without hesitation.

Each act felt like a tiny offering, like laying a gift before Jesus. And as the day went on, she noticed something surprising—giving felt good. It filled her heart with joy, the kind that came not from getting something, but from giving something back.

THAT EVENING, AS CHLOE helped her mom set up the nativity scene for the church, she carefully placed the wise men in their spots. She looked at the tiny figures, each holding their precious treasure, and smiled.

"What are you thinking about?" her mom asked, noticing her quiet expression.

Chloe shrugged, a shy smile on her face. "I was just thinking that I might not have gold or frankincense or myrrh, but I think I've found some gifts I can give to Jesus."

Her mom crouched beside her, her eyes full of love. "I think He's going to love them, Chloe. More than you know."

Day 16 - The Promise Fulfilled

The air was crisp and still as the snow outside Abby's window glistened under the soft glow of the Christmas lights. Inside, the living room was warm and cozy, filled with the scent of pine and the soft hum of Christmas carols playing in the background. Abby sat curled up in the corner of the couch, a blanket draped over her lap, and her Bible resting open beside her. She traced her finger along the words her mom had read aloud earlier during their family devotion time:

"But thou, Bethlehem Ephratah, though thou be little among the thousands of Judah, yet out of thee shall he come forth unto me that is to be ruler in Israel; whose goings forth have been from of old, from everlasting." (Micah 5:2)

The verse lingered in Abby's mind. It spoke of a promise God had made long ago, that the Savior would come from Bethlehem—a promise fulfilled when Jesus was born in a stable on that first Christmas night.

Abby turned to her mom, who sat nearby knitting a scarf. "Mom," she asked, her voice thoughtful, "why did God make a promise about Bethlehem? It's such a small place. Couldn't He have picked somewhere bigger?"

Her mom set her knitting aside, her eyes warm with the kind of wisdom that always calmed Abby's wondering heart. "That's a great question, Abby," she said. "Bethlehem was small and humble, just like the stable where Jesus was born. By choosing Bethlehem, God was showing us that He often uses ordinary places and people to do extraordinary things."

ABBY THOUGHT ABOUT that for a moment, her imagination carrying her back in time to a quiet village in the hills of Judah. She pictured shepherds leading their flocks through rocky pastures, the streets of Bethlehem dusty and bustling with travelers. It wasn't a grand city like Jerusalem, but it was the place God had chosen for His greatest promise to be fulfilled.

"Did the people know about the promise?" Abby asked. "Did they know the Savior was going to be born there?"

Her mom nodded. "Some of them did. Prophets like Micah and Isaiah had written about the Savior's coming hundreds of years earlier. The people were waiting for Him, hoping for the day when God would send the One who would save them. But I think many of them didn't expect it to happen the way it did."

ABBY IMAGINED WHAT it must have been like to wait for so long. She thought about the people of Israel, living under Roman rule, longing for a King who would bring peace and freedom. Did they picture someone powerful, riding in on a horse with an army behind Him? Did they ever expect that God's plan would begin in a stable, with a tiny baby wrapped in swaddling clothes?

Her mom seemed to read her thoughts. "God's promises don't always come in the way we expect, Abby," she said. "But they always come true. Jesus' birth was the fulfillment of every promise God had made to His people. It showed that God is faithful—that He always keeps His word."

ABBY CLOSED HER EYES, letting her mom's words sink in. She thought about the story she'd heard so many times—the angel appearing to Mary, the journey to Bethlehem, the star shining brightly over the stable. It was more than just a story. It was proof that God's promises were real.

She opened her eyes and looked at the nativity scene on the mantle. The tiny figure of baby Jesus lay in the manger, surrounded by Mary, Joseph, the shepherds, and the wise men. For the first time, Abby saw it not just as a decoration, but as a reminder that God's promises had come true.

"Mom," she said softly, "do you think God's still making promises to us today?"

Her mom smiled, her eyes shining with gentle pride. "I do, Abby. The Bible is full of God's promises—promises that are just as true for us now as they were back then. He promises to love us, to guide us, to be with us no matter what.

And just like He fulfilled His promise to send Jesus, He'll keep those promises too."

LATER THAT NIGHT, ABBY sat at her desk, the glow of her bedside lamp illuminating her journal. She opened to a blank page and wrote at the top: God's Promises. Below it, she began to list the ones she could remember:
- God loves me.
- God is always with me.
- God forgives me.
- God has a plan for me.

She paused, her pen hovering over the page. "God keeps His promises," she whispered, adding the words to the bottom of the list.

IN HER MIND, SHE PICTURED Mary and Joseph arriving in Bethlehem, weary from their journey. She imagined them hearing the innkeeper's words—"no room"—and yet finding a humble stable where the greatest promise of all would be fulfilled. She thought about the shepherds, kneeling in awe, and the wise men, bringing their gifts. They were witnesses to God's faithfulness, each one drawn into the story of a promise kept.

Before climbing into bed, Abby knelt by her window, looking out at the clear, starry sky. She whispered a quiet prayer, her heart full of wonder. "Thank You, God, for keeping Your promise to send Jesus. Help me to trust Your promises, even when I don't understand Your plans."

THE NEXT MORNING, AS Abby helped her mom make breakfast, she thought about how she could share the story of God's promises with others. She decided to start small—writing a card for her neighbor, Mrs. Thompson, who lived alone, and offering to help her dad shovel the driveway without being asked. Each act felt like a way of saying, "God keeps His promises," through kindness and love.

That evening, as she read her Bible by the fire, Abby came across another verse that made her smile. It was from Isaiah, another prophet who had spoken of Jesus long before He was born: "For unto us a child is born, unto us a son is given: and the government shall be upon his shoulder: and his name shall be called Wonderful, Counsellor, The mighty God, The everlasting Father, The Prince of Peace." (Isaiah 9:6)

Abby underlined the verse, her heart swelling with gratitude. Jesus was the fulfillment of God's promises—a reminder of His unchanging faithfulness.

AS CHRISTMAS DREW CLOSER, Abby carried the lesson with her, finding ways to share the hope of God's promises with everyone around her. And each time she saw the nativity scene, she felt a quiet joy, knowing that it was more than just a story—it was a promise fulfilled.

Day 17 - The Message of Peace

The classroom was alive with the hum of children's voices as they finished making paper angel crafts. Glitter and glue sticks were scattered across the tables, and the faint scent of freshly sharpened pencils lingered in the air. At the front of the room, Miss Clara clapped her hands to get their attention.

"All right, everyone," she said with a warm smile. "It's time for our special story. Today, Daniel has something to share with us about the angels' message on the night Jesus was born."

Daniel, a quiet boy with bright eyes, stepped to the front of the room, holding a small card with his notes. He glanced nervously at his classmates but took a deep breath, encouraged by Miss Clara's reassuring nod.

"Hi, everyone," he began, his voice steady but soft. "I'm going to talk about the angels' message of peace—the one they gave to the shepherds. It's my favorite part of the Christmas story because it shows that Jesus came to bring peace to everyone."

DANIEL PAUSED, GLANCING at the nativity scene set up on a small table beside him. He pointed to the tiny figures of the shepherds, who stood near their sheep. "The Bible says that the shepherds were out in the fields at night, watching over their flocks, when an angel appeared to them. They were really scared because the angel was so bright and glorious."

He looked up, his voice gaining confidence. "But the angel said, 'Fear not: for, behold, I bring you good tidings of great joy, which shall be to all people.' Then the angel told them about Jesus, and suddenly, the sky was filled with a whole choir of angels. They were praising God and saying, 'Glory to God in the highest, and on earth peace, good will toward men.'"

The room was quiet as the children imagined the scene—a hillside bathed in heavenly light, the sky alive with the sound of angelic voices.

DANIEL CONTINUED, HIS expression thoughtful. "What's really amazing to me is that the angels said the message of peace was for all people. Not just the rich or important people, but everyone—even the shepherds, who were just ordinary workers. It shows that Jesus didn't come just for a few people—He came to bring peace to the whole world."

Miss Clara nodded, her smile encouraging. "That's a wonderful thought, Daniel. What do you think the angels meant by 'peace'?"

Daniel paused, considering the question. "I think they meant more than just not fighting," he said slowly. "They meant a kind of peace that fills your heart—peace with God, peace with others, and even peace with yourself."

AS DANIEL SPOKE, HE thought about how much the world needed peace. He remembered the times he had fought with his younger sister over toys or felt nervous about tests at school. He thought about the news reports he'd overheard on TV, talking about wars and people arguing with each other. The world felt so big and full of problems sometimes, but the angels' message reminded him that Jesus had come to bring hope.

"Jesus is called the Prince of Peace," Daniel said, his voice growing stronger. "When He was born, He brought a peace that's deeper than anything we can find on our own. It's a peace that comes from knowing God loves us and that we're never alone."

THE CHILDREN LISTENED intently, their glitter-covered angel crafts forgotten for the moment. One of the younger boys raised his hand. "But how can we have peace if people are still fighting?"

Daniel nodded, understanding the question. "I think peace starts small," he said. "It starts in our hearts when we trust Jesus. And then it spreads, like ripples in a pond. When we have peace with God, we can share it with others by being kind, forgiving, and showing love."

Miss Clara beamed. "That's a beautiful answer, Daniel. Peace isn't something we just wait for—it's something we live out, just like Jesus taught us."

DANIEL SMILED, FEELING more confident now. "The angels' message wasn't just for the shepherds," he said. "It's for us too. When we celebrate Christmas, we're celebrating the peace Jesus brings. And we can be part of spreading that peace in our own lives."

Miss Clara clapped her hands lightly. "Thank you, Daniel. That was a wonderful reminder of what Christmas is all about."

LATER THAT EVENING, Daniel sat by the window in his room, looking out at the clear, starry sky. He imagined the hills of Bethlehem, quiet and dark, and the shepherds staring in amazement as the angels filled the night with light and song. He tried to picture what it must have felt like to hear those words: "Glory to God in the highest, and on earth peace, good will toward men."

He thought about what Miss Clara had said—that peace isn't just something we wait for, but something we live out. He wondered how he could share peace in his own little corner of the world.

THE NEXT MORNING, DANIEL put his thoughts into action. When his sister spilled juice all over the kitchen table, instead of getting annoyed, he helped her clean it up. At school, when his friend Lucas felt left out during a game, Daniel invited him to join. Each small act felt like a way of sharing the peace Jesus had brought to the world.

That night, as Daniel knelt by his bed to pray, he whispered, "Thank You, Jesus, for bringing peace to the world. Help me to live in Your peace and share it with others."

OVER THE DAYS LEADING up to Christmas, Daniel carried the angels' message with him. He found joy in simple things—helping his mom bake cookies for their neighbors, making cards for friends, and spending time with his family. Each act felt like a little reflection of the heavenly peace the angels had announced so long ago.

And on Christmas Eve, as Daniel sat with his family in church, singing carols by candlelight, he felt a deep, quiet joy in his heart. The angels' message wasn't just a story—it was a promise, one that he could live out every day.

Day 18 - Jesus, Immanuel: God With Us

The sanctuary glowed with the soft light of candles, their flames flickering gently as a hush fell over the children seated on colorful cushions in front of the altar. The scent of evergreen branches mingled with the faint aroma of the old wood pews. Pastor John stood before the group, his Bible open in his hands, his kind eyes scanning the eager faces. He loved moments like these, when he could share not only the beauty of the Christmas story but the deeper truths that came with it.

"Do you all know what the name 'Immanuel' means?" Pastor John asked, his voice warm and inviting.

A few hands shot up. Abby was the first to speak. "It means 'God with us,' right?"

"Exactly," Pastor John said with a smile. "But do you know why that name is so important? Why it's one of the most amazing things we can celebrate at Christmas?"

The children exchanged curious glances, shaking their heads.

"Let me tell you a story," Pastor John began, closing his Bible gently. "It's not just a story about Jesus' birth—it's a story about how everything changed when God chose to come and be with us."

PASTOR JOHN WALKED over to the nativity scene set up near the altar. The children followed his gaze to the tiny figures of Mary, Joseph, and baby Jesus, surrounded by shepherds and animals.

"Long before Jesus was born, the people of Israel were waiting for a Savior," he said. "They had heard the prophecies, like the one in Isaiah, that said, 'Behold, a virgin shall be with child, and shall bring forth a son, and they shall call his name Immanuel, which being interpreted is, God with us.'"

He paused, letting the words sink in. "But what does it mean for God to be with us? Think about it for a moment. God, the Creator of everything—the stars, the oceans, the mountains—chose to come down and live among us. He didn't stay far away in heaven. He came close."

BEN RAISED HIS HAND, his brow furrowed in thought. "But why did He have to come close? Couldn't He just fix everything from heaven?"

Pastor John nodded, his expression serious but kind. "That's a great question, Ben. God could have stayed in heaven, but He wanted us to know Him in a personal way. By coming as Jesus, God showed us His love in a way we could see, hear, and understand. He walked where we walk, felt what we feel, and lived as one of us."

Abby's eyes widened. "So, when Jesus was born, it was like God saying, 'I'm here with you'?"

"Exactly," Pastor John said, his smile returning. "And not just for the people in Bethlehem, but for all of us—for everyone, everywhere, and for all time. That's what Immanuel means: God with us, not far away or out of reach, but right here in our lives."

AS PASTOR JOHN SPOKE, the children could almost picture the scene: the quiet hills of Bethlehem, the stable filled with the earthy scent of hay and the soft sounds of animals. They imagined Mary holding baby Jesus, her face full of wonder, while Joseph stood close by, protective and proud. In that tiny manger lay not just a baby, but God Himself, come to be with His people.

"BUT JESUS DIDN'T STAY a baby," Pastor John continued, drawing the children's attention back to him. "He grew up, just like you're growing up now. He played, He learned, and eventually, He began to teach people about God's kingdom. He healed the sick, comforted the hurting, and showed everyone what God's love looks like."

He paused, his voice softening. "And then, Jesus did something even greater. He gave His life for us on the cross, taking away our sin so we could be with God forever. That's the ultimate meaning of 'God with us.' He didn't just come to visit—He came to save."

CHLOE RAISED HER HAND, her expression thoughtful. "So, does that mean Jesus is still with us now, even though He's not here like He was back then?"

"Yes, Chloe," Pastor John said, his voice filled with joy. "When Jesus returned to heaven after His resurrection, He promised something amazing. He said, 'I am with you always, even unto the end of the world.' Through His Spirit, Jesus is still with us today—in our hearts, in our lives, and in everything we do."

THE CHILDREN SAT QUIETLY for a moment, their faces reflecting a mixture of awe and understanding. Ben broke the silence, his voice soft but clear. "So, if Jesus is always with us, that means we're never really alone, right?"

"That's exactly right, Ben," Pastor John said. "No matter where we are or what we're going through, Jesus is with us. When we're happy, He's with us. When we're sad or scared, He's with us. Immanuel means we can always trust that God is near."

AFTER THE LESSON, THE children worked together to make ornaments shaped like stars, each one decorated with the word "Immanuel" in glittery letters. As they worked, their conversations buzzed with excitement.

"I think it's so cool that Jesus came to be with us," Chloe said as she carefully placed a golden star on her ornament. "It makes Christmas feel even more special."

"Yeah," Ben agreed. "It's like God saying, 'I'll never leave you.'"

THAT EVENING, AS ABBY sat by the Christmas tree at home, she thought about what Pastor John had said. She stared at the star on top of the tree, its light casting soft shadows on the walls. She thought about Jesus, the tiny baby in the manger, who came not just to live among His people, but to save them.

She closed her eyes and whispered a quiet prayer. "Thank You, Jesus, for being with us. Thank You for loving us so much that You came to be part of our world. Help me to always remember that You're with me, no matter what."

OVER THE NEXT FEW DAYS, the lesson of Immanuel stayed with Abby and the other children. They found ways to live out what they had learned—by helping their families prepare for Christmas, sharing kind words with friends, and reaching out to those who needed encouragement. Each act felt like a small reflection of the love that Jesus, Immanuel, had brought into the world.

And as Christmas Eve arrived, Abby looked at the nativity scene one last time before bed. She smiled, her heart full of peace. The name Immanuel wasn't just a name—it was a promise. A promise that God was with them then, now, and always.

Day 19 - Mary Ponders These Things

The quiet stillness of the winter evening wrapped around Abby's home like a comforting blanket. Snow covered the ground outside, muffling all sound except the faint rustling of wind through the trees. Abby sat on the couch by the fire, a fuzzy blanket draped over her legs and a mug of hot cocoa warming her hands. Across from her, her mom was flipping through a book of Christmas devotionals.

"Mom," Abby asked, breaking the silence, "what does it mean that Mary 'kept all these things and pondered them in her heart'? Miss Clara read that verse in Sunday school today, and I can't stop thinking about it."

Her mom looked up from her book, her eyes soft and thoughtful. "That's a beautiful verse, Abby," she said. "It shows us how much Mary treasured everything that happened around Jesus' birth. She didn't just let those moments pass by—she kept them close, thinking about what they meant."

"But what kinds of things was she thinking about?" Abby asked, curiosity lighting up her face.

Her mom set the book aside and leaned forward, resting her chin on her hand. "Let's think about all that Mary had experienced. She'd been visited by an angel who told her she would have a very special child—the Son of God. She'd traveled to Bethlehem while expecting a baby, only to give birth in a stable. And then, just when she might have felt alone, shepherds showed up, saying that angels had appeared to them, announcing Jesus' birth."

Abby's imagination came alive as her mom spoke. She could picture Mary sitting in the dim light of the stable, holding baby Jesus in her arms, her face glowing with a mix of joy and wonder. She imagined the shepherds kneeling nearby, their rough hands trembling as they offered quiet words of praise.

"MARY MUST HAVE FELT so many things all at once," her mom continued. "She knew her baby was the Savior, but she didn't know yet what that would mean. She must have thought about all the ways God had worked to bring her to that moment, and she treasured those memories in her heart."

Abby tilted her head, thinking. "So, it's like she was keeping a journal in her heart? Writing everything down so she wouldn't forget?"

Her mom smiled. "That's a great way to think about it. Mary didn't have all the answers yet, but she trusted God's plan. By pondering everything in her heart, she was showing her faith and her gratitude for what God was doing."

ABBY STARED AT THE fire, the flames dancing in the hearth. She imagined Mary years later, remembering that night in Bethlehem—the angels' song, the shepherds' joy, and the tiny baby asleep in the manger. How had those memories shaped her, Abby wondered? How could she, like Mary, treasure Jesus in her own heart?

Her mom seemed to sense her thoughts. "You know," she said gently, "we can learn a lot from Mary. She teaches us to slow down and really think about what Jesus' birth means. It's not just a story we hear at Christmas—it's the story of God's love for us. And when we take time to treasure that, it changes us."

LATER THAT EVENING, Abby sat at her desk, her journal open before her. She picked up her pen and wrote at the top of the page: "Things I Want to Treasure in My Heart." For a moment, she stared at the blank space, unsure where to start. Then she closed her eyes and thought about the nativity scene she had helped her mom set up earlier that day.

IN HER MIND, THE STABLE came to life. She saw Mary sitting on a bed of hay, her arms cradling baby Jesus. The shepherds were gathered around, their faces lit with awe, while Joseph stood close by, his protective gaze resting on his small family. The soft glow of the lantern cast long shadows on the walls, and the gentle bleating of sheep filled the air.

Abby imagined Mary looking down at her son, her heart full of wonder. Who would He grow up to be? How would He save the world? The answers weren't clear yet, but one thing was certain: God's promise had come true, and His love was here.

OPENING HER EYES, ABBY began to write.

- Jesus was born to save us. God kept His promise.

- God's love is for everyone, just like the angels said.

- Jesus came humbly, born in a stable. That shows how much He cares about all of us.

She paused, tapping the pen against her chin. Then she wrote one more line: I want to treasure Jesus in my heart, just like Mary did.

THE NEXT MORNING, ABBY decided to put her thoughts into action. She asked her mom if they could bake cookies for their neighbor, Mrs. Peterson, who had been feeling lonely. As they worked together in the kitchen, Abby felt a quiet joy in her heart. It wasn't just about the cookies—it was about showing love, the way Jesus had shown love by coming into the world.

Later, when her little brother, Ben, spilled his toys all over the living room, Abby surprised herself by helping him clean up instead of scolding him. Each small act felt like a way of treasuring Jesus, a reminder of the love He had brought into her life.

THAT NIGHT, AS SHE lay in bed, Abby looked out her window at the clear, starry sky. She thought about Mary again, holding baby Jesus and pondering all the ways God was at work. Abby whispered a quiet prayer, her heart full of gratitude.

"Thank You, Jesus, for coming to be with us. Help me to treasure You in my heart every day."

OVER THE NEXT FEW DAYS, Abby continued to reflect on Mary's example. She wrote in her journal each evening, listing moments where she had felt God's love or seen ways to share it with others. The more she wrote, the more she realized how much she had to be thankful for—and how much she wanted to keep those memories close.

By the time Christmas morning arrived, Abby's heart felt like it was overflowing. She sat by the tree with her family, opening presents and laughing together, but the greatest gift she felt was the one she couldn't see: the presence of Jesus, treasured in her heart.

Day 20 - God's Light in the Darkness

The living room was dimly lit, the only source of light coming from the soft glow of the Christmas tree and the flickering candles on the mantle. Snow fell gently outside the window, adding a hushed stillness to the evening. Ben sat cross-legged on the floor, his eyes fixed on the tiny star perched atop the tree. Beside him sat his cousin Jonah, who was busy arranging the figures of the nativity scene on the coffee table.

Their uncle David, with his warm smile and deep voice, was seated on the couch, holding a mug of hot cocoa. He had just finished telling a funny story about one of his childhood Christmases, but now his tone grew more serious as he leaned forward.

"Do you boys know why the star on top of the tree is so important?" Uncle David asked.

Ben glanced at Jonah, who shrugged before turning back to their uncle. "Because it's part of the Christmas story?" Ben guessed.

"That's right," Uncle David said. "But it's more than just part of the story—it's a symbol. The star reminds us of something incredible: that when Jesus was born, He brought light into a dark world."

BEN TILTED HIS HEAD, intrigued. "What do you mean by 'dark world'? Was it nighttime when Jesus was born?"

Uncle David chuckled softly. "Yes, it was night, but that's not the kind of darkness I'm talking about. The world was full of spiritual darkness—people were lost, hurting, and far away from God. They needed someone to guide them, to bring them hope. That's why Jesus came. He said, 'I am the light of the world: he that followeth me shall not walk in darkness, but shall have the light of life.'"

Ben leaned forward, his curiosity growing. "So the star in the sky was like a sign?"

"Exactly," Uncle David said. "It was a beacon, shining brightly to show the wise men where to find Jesus. But it was also a reminder that Jesus Himself is the light we all need. He came to shine into the darkest places and bring us closer to God."

IN BEN'S MIND, THE story began to unfold. He imagined the wise men standing in a quiet desert, their eyes fixed on the night sky. Among the countless stars twinkling above, one shone brighter than all the others, its glow steady and pure. It seemed to call to them, urging them forward on their journey.

"The wise men followed the star for miles and miles," Uncle David continued. "They didn't know exactly where it would lead, but they trusted that it would bring them to something wonderful. And it did—it brought them to Jesus, the Savior."

BEN STARED AT THE STAR on top of the tree, its golden light reflecting off the ornaments. "But what does it mean for us?" he asked. "Jesus isn't here like He was back then. How is He still the light?"

Uncle David's expression grew thoughtful. "That's a good question, Ben. Jesus is still the light because He helps us see what's true and right. He shows us how to live with love, kindness, and forgiveness. When we follow Him, we don't have to be afraid of the dark—whether it's the darkness in the world or the worries in our own hearts."

Jonah looked up from the nativity scene, his face serious. "So, it's like He's a guide?"

"Exactly," Uncle David said. "Just like the star guided the wise men, Jesus guides us. And when we trust Him, His light shines in us too. That's how we can share His love with others—by being little lights in the world."

BEN SAT BACK, LETTING the words sink in. He thought about the times he had felt scared or unsure, like when he had to give a presentation in school or when he'd gotten lost at the park last summer. In those moments, he had prayed, asking Jesus to help him, and each time, he'd felt a sense of calm, as if a light had broken through the darkness.

"So, we can be lights too?" he asked.

"Yes," Uncle David said, his smile widening. "When we choose to follow Jesus, we reflect His light. It's like holding up a mirror to the sun—the light doesn't come from us, but we can share it with the people around us."

THE ROOM GREW QUIET for a moment, the soft crackling of the fire filling the silence. Then Uncle David leaned forward again, his voice low and steady.

"Do you boys want to know something amazing?" he asked.

Ben and Jonah nodded eagerly.

"The same God who placed that star in the sky to lead the wise men," Uncle David said, "is still placing lights in the world today. Sometimes those lights are people, like pastors or friends who point us to Jesus. And sometimes those lights are moments, like when we hear a song or read a verse in the Bible that reminds us of God's love. No matter what form it takes, God's light is always shining, leading us closer to Him."

LATER THAT NIGHT, AFTER Uncle David had left and the house had grown quiet, Ben lay in bed, staring at the glow-in-the-dark stars on his ceiling. He thought about the star of Bethlehem, its brilliance cutting through the night, and the wise men, faithfully following its light.

"Jesus," he whispered into the darkness, "thank You for being the light of the world. Help me to follow You, even when things feel dark. And help me to share Your light with others."

THE NEXT MORNING, BEN woke up with a sense of purpose. As he got ready for the day, he looked for small ways to reflect Jesus' light. When his little sister needed help tying her shoes, he knelt down and showed her how. When his mom asked for help carrying groceries inside, he volunteered without hesitation. Each act felt like a tiny spark, a way of sharing the light that had been shared with him.

That evening, as the family gathered around the tree to sing Christmas carols, Ben's heart was full. He looked at the star on top of the tree one last time, its golden glow casting soft shadows on the walls. It wasn't just a decoration—it was a reminder. A reminder that even in the darkest moments, God's light was shining, leading the way.

Day 21 - Shepherds Share the Good News

The soft hum of excitement filled the church basement as the children gathered for their Christmas play rehearsal. The stage was small but lovingly decorated with hay bales, a makeshift stable, and a twinkling backdrop of stars. Chloe adjusted her shepherd's robe, her fingers nervously fiddling with the edge of the fabric. She and the other children were about to act out the moment when the shepherds ran to tell everyone about baby Jesus.

Miss Clara, their Sunday school teacher, stood in front of the stage with her clipboard, her warm smile encouraging the children to focus. "All right, everyone," she said. "Remember, this scene is all about the shepherds sharing the good news. They've just seen something incredible—the Savior of the world—and they can't keep it to themselves. Ready?"

The children nodded, their faces eager.

"Great," Miss Clara said. "Let's start with the angels appearing to the shepherds. Chloe, you're first. Step forward when you hear the angel's message."

CHLOE TOOK A DEEP BREATH as the scene began. The room dimmed, and a spotlight shone on the group of children dressed as shepherds. They huddled around a fake campfire, their plastic sheep scattered at their feet. A recording of soft, angelic music played in the background, and then the voice of the "angel" boomed from the speakers.

"Fear not: for, behold, I bring you good tidings of great joy, which shall be to all people. For unto you is born this day in the city of David a Savior, which is Christ the Lord."

Chloe looked up, her face mimicking awe as the angel's message continued. When the recording ended, the spotlight expanded to include the other shepherds. Chloe stepped forward, her voice steady as she delivered her line.

"Let us go to Bethlehem and see this thing which has come to pass, which the Lord hath made known unto us."

The children playing shepherds nodded and pretended to gather their sheep. They "ran" to the stable on the other side of the stage, where Mary and Joseph waited with a doll wrapped in a blanket. The music swelled as the shepherds knelt before the manger, their faces full of wonder.

AFTER A MOMENT OF SILENT reverence, the shepherds stood. This was Chloe's favorite part—the moment when the shepherds became messengers.

"Let's go tell everyone what we've seen," Chloe said, her voice filled with excitement.

The shepherds scattered across the stage, pretending to knock on doors and talk to invisible townspeople. One by one, they delivered their lines, their voices growing more animated with each repetition.

"We've seen the Savior!" one boy shouted.

"The angels told us the good news—He's here!" another added.

The stage came alive with movement and energy, the children acting out the shepherds' joy and urgency. Chloe felt a thrill as she pretended to tell the townspeople about Jesus. She imagined what it must have been like for the real shepherds—ordinary people who had experienced something extraordinary and couldn't wait to share it.

WHEN THE SCENE ENDED, Miss Clara clapped her hands, her face beaming with pride. "Wonderful job, everyone! That was fantastic."

The children grinned, their nervousness replaced by excitement. Chloe joined the others on the floor, her heart still racing from the performance. She couldn't help but think about what it must have been like for the shepherds that night.

Miss Clara stepped forward, her clipboard tucked under her arm. "Now that we've acted out the story, let's talk about it for a moment," she said. "Why do you think the shepherds were so eager to tell everyone about what they saw?"

One of the younger boys raised his hand. "Because it was exciting?"

Miss Clara nodded. "Yes, it was very exciting. But it was more than that. The shepherds knew they had witnessed something life-changing. They understood that the baby in the manger was the Savior, the one God had promised to send. They wanted everyone to know about Him."

CHLOE RAISED HER HAND. "So, they were like the first messengers?"

"Exactly," Miss Clara said, smiling. "The shepherds were the first to share the good news of Jesus' birth. And their story reminds us that we can do the same. When we know about Jesus and His love, we have the chance to share that good news with others."

Ben, who had been quietly watching from the back, raised his hand. "But what if we don't know what to say? The shepherds had angels to tell them what happened. We don't."

"That's a great question, Ben," Miss Clara said. "The good news doesn't have to be complicated. The shepherds didn't give long speeches—they simply told people what they had seen and heard. We can do the same by sharing how Jesus has made a difference in our lives or by showing His love through our actions."

AS THE CHILDREN THOUGHT about her words, Miss Clara handed out small slips of paper with the words "Good News" written across the top. "I want you to take a moment to think about how you can share the good news of Jesus with someone this week," she said. "It could be through a kind word, a thoughtful gesture, or even just telling someone about the true meaning of Christmas."

Chloe stared at the slip of paper, her mind racing with ideas. She thought about her neighbor, Mrs. Wilson, who lived alone and always seemed so quiet and lonely. Maybe she could visit her and bring some cookies. Or she could write a card for her teacher, thanking her for all she did. Each idea felt small, but it also felt important—like a way of sharing the joy she had felt on stage that night.

THAT EVENING, AS CHLOE sat by the Christmas tree at home, she wrote down her plan on the slip of paper. She decided to make a card for Mrs. Wilson and deliver it with a plate of cookies. As she worked, she thought about the shepherds running through the streets of Bethlehem, their voices filled with excitement as they shared the good news.

"Jesus," she prayed softly, "help me to be like the shepherds. Help me to share Your love with others."

THE NEXT DAY, CHLOE and her mom walked over to Mrs. Wilson's house, the card and cookies in hand. Mrs. Wilson's face lit up when she opened the door, her eyes shining with gratitude as she accepted the gift.

"This means so much to me, Chloe," she said, her voice trembling slightly. "Thank you for thinking of me."

As they walked back home, Chloe felt a warmth in her heart. She realized that sharing the good news didn't have to be hard or scary—it could be as simple as showing kindness and letting others know they were loved.

ON CHRISTMAS EVE, DURING the church service, Chloe stood with the other children and sang "Go Tell It on the Mountain." Her voice was steady and strong, her heart full of joy as she thought about the shepherds and their message.

As the final notes of the song echoed through the sanctuary, Chloe whispered a prayer. "Thank You, Jesus, for being the good news we all need. Help me to keep sharing Your love, just like the shepherds did."

Day 22 - The Savior for All People

The gentle hum of conversation filled the church fellowship hall, where families had gathered for the annual Christmas potluck. The tables were lined with red and green tablecloths, dotted with platters of cookies, bowls of mashed potatoes, and trays of roasted turkey. Daniel sat near the end of one table, a paper plate of food in front of him, but he wasn't eating. His eyes were fixed on the large banner hanging above the stage at the far end of the room. In bold letters, it read:

"For God so loved the world, that he gave his only begotten Son, that whosoever believeth in him should not perish, but have everlasting life."

—John 3:16

Daniel read the words over and over, his mind turning them over like a puzzle. The phrase "loved the world" felt so big, so vast. He had always known that Jesus came to save people, but this verse made it clear: Jesus came for everyone.

"DANIEL," A VOICE INTERRUPTED his thoughts. He looked up to see his dad sitting down beside him, a plate of food in his hands. "You look deep in thought. What's on your mind?"

Daniel gestured toward the banner. "I was just thinking about how it says God loved the world. That means Jesus came for everyone, right? Not just the people in Bethlehem or the people back then, but the whole world?"

His dad smiled, nodding. "That's exactly what it means, Daniel. Jesus didn't come for just one group of people—He came for everyone, everywhere, no matter where they're from or what they've done. That's the amazing thing about God's love: it's for all of us."

AS THEY SAT TOGETHER, Daniel's dad began to tell the Christmas story from a new angle. "Think about the people who were there the night Jesus was born," he said. "The first to hear the news were the shepherds—ordinary people, not rich or powerful. Then later, the wise men came from faraway lands, people who didn't even worship the same God. But they all came to see Jesus, because He was the Savior for everyone."

Daniel imagined the scene in his mind. He saw the shepherds, their faces still lit with awe from the angels' message, hurrying to the stable to see the baby. He saw the wise men, dressed in rich robes, bowing low before Jesus, their gifts of gold, frankincense, and myrrh glinting in the lantern light. Each person was so different, but they were all drawn to the same Savior.

"THAT'S WHY WE HAVE verses like John 3:16," his dad continued, pointing to the banner. "It's a reminder that God's love isn't limited by borders or cultures. It's for every person, every family, and every nation. And it's a love so big that God sent His Son to save us all."

Daniel frowned thoughtfully. "But what about people who don't know about Jesus? Or people who don't believe in Him? Does God still love them?"

His dad's expression grew tender. "Yes, Daniel. God's love is unconditional. He loves everyone, even those who don't know Him yet. That's why it's so important for us to share the good news. When we tell others about Jesus, we're helping them see the light of His love."

THE CONVERSATION STAYED with Daniel long after the potluck ended. That night, as he sat in his room, he stared at the nativity scene on his dresser. The tiny figures of Mary, Joseph, the shepherds, and the wise men seemed to echo what his dad had said—different people from different places, all coming together to worship the same Savior.

Daniel opened his Bible and flipped to John 3:16. He read the verse aloud to himself, the words filling the quiet room:

"For God so loved the world, that He gave His only begotten Son, that whosoever believeth in Him should not perish, but have everlasting life."

He paused, focusing on the word "whosoever." It didn't say "just the good people" or "only the people from Bethlehem." It said whosoever. That meant everyone—his classmates at school, his neighbors down the street, even people on the other side of the world.

THE NEXT DAY, DANIEL decided to share what he had learned. During Sunday school, Miss Clara asked the children what Christmas meant to them. When it was Daniel's turn, he stood up, his heart pounding a little but his voice steady.

"Christmas is about Jesus coming to save everyone," he said. "Not just one group of people, but the whole world. That's what John 3:16 says—that God loved the world so much, He gave His Son for all of us. And because of that, we can share His love with others."

Miss Clara's face lit up with a smile. "That's a beautiful answer, Daniel. You're absolutely right—Christmas is about God's love for the whole world. And when we celebrate Jesus' birth, we're celebrating that amazing love."

LATER THAT WEEK, DANIEL found ways to share the love of Jesus in simple, everyday moments. He helped his mom make sandwiches for the local shelter and prayed for the people who would receive them. At school, he included a new student in his group during art class, even though the boy seemed shy and unsure. And when his little sister asked him to read her a bedtime story, he chose one about Jesus, explaining why His birth was the greatest gift of all.

Each act, no matter how small, felt like a way of reflecting the love that had been shown to him. Daniel thought about the shepherds and the wise men again—how they had responded to Jesus by worshiping Him and sharing the good news. He realized he could do the same in his own way.

ON CHRISTMAS EVE, DANIEL sat with his family in the pews of their church, the sanctuary glowing with the light of hundreds of candles. As the congregation sang "Silent Night," Daniel's thoughts returned to John 3:16. He pictured the shepherds running through the streets of Bethlehem, telling everyone they could find about the Savior. He imagined the wise men, their long journey finally ending as they knelt before Jesus. Each one was part of the same story—a story that spanned the entire world.

When the song ended, Daniel bowed his head and whispered a quiet prayer. "Thank You, God, for sending Jesus to save all of us. Help me to share Your love, so everyone can know how much You care for them."

Day 23 - God Chooses the Humble

The soft glow of the Christmas tree filled the living room as Abby sat on the couch, her Bible open on her lap. Snow fell gently outside the window, and the quiet hum of Christmas carols played from a speaker nearby. Her family had just finished their nightly Advent devotion, but Abby lingered, flipping through the pages of her Bible.

Her eyes landed on a verse from James: "Humble yourselves in the sight of the Lord, and He shall lift you up." (James 4:10)

She read the words again, her heart stirring. "Mom," she said, looking up, "why does God choose humble people? Like the shepherds or the stable? Why not something grander?"

Her mom, seated nearby with her own Bible, smiled. "That's a wonderful question, Abby. God often chooses the humble to show us that His power doesn't depend on worldly things like wealth, status, or strength. It's His way of reminding us that He works through those who trust Him, no matter how small or ordinary they might seem."

Abby nodded thoughtfully, her mind swirling with images of the Christmas story. The shepherds, the stable, and even Mary and Joseph—they weren't rich or powerful. Yet God had chosen them to be part of the greatest event in history.

LATER THAT EVENING, Abby sat at her desk, her journal open in front of her. She picked up her pen and began to write:

God chose the shepherds to hear the angels' message. He chose a stable for Jesus to be born. Why does He choose the humble? Because He wants us to see that it's about His greatness, not ours.

As she wrote, her imagination carried her back to that night in Bethlehem. She pictured the hills where the shepherds watched over their sheep, the sky suddenly filled with the glorious light of angels. The shepherds were ordinary people, often overlooked and ignored, but God had chosen them to hear the good news first.

IN HER MIND, THE SCENE unfolded. The shepherds stood in stunned silence as the angel spoke: "Fear not: for, behold, I bring you good tidings of great joy, which shall be to all people." The angel's voice was steady and kind, filled with a joy that seemed to pour over the hills like sunlight.

Abby imagined how the shepherds must have felt—unworthy, amazed, and yet deeply honored. God hadn't sent the angels to kings or priests. He had chosen them, the humble caretakers of sheep, to be the first witnesses of the Savior's birth.

She pictured the shepherds running to Bethlehem, their hearts pounding with excitement. When they arrived at the stable, they found Mary, Joseph, and baby Jesus lying in a manger. The stable was simple and quiet, with the earthy scent of hay and the soft rustling of animals. Yet in that unassuming place, God had done something extraordinary.

AS ABBY WROTE IN HER journal, she thought about what the stable represented. It wasn't grand or luxurious. It was humble, just like the people God had chosen to be there. And yet, it had become the setting for the most important birth in history.

Abby's pen moved quickly across the page. The stable reminds us that God doesn't need fancy places to do amazing things. He can take the ordinary and make it extraordinary.

THE NEXT MORNING, ABBY decided to share her thoughts with her Sunday school class. As the children gathered in the small classroom, Miss Clara smiled and gestured for Abby to come to the front.

"Abby has something special to share with us today," Miss Clara said. "She's been thinking about the shepherds and the stable and what they teach us about God's plans."

Abby took a deep breath, her hands gripping the edges of her notebook. She looked out at her classmates, who were watching her with curious expressions.

"Hi, everyone," she began, her voice steady but soft. "I've been thinking about why God chose the shepherds to hear the angels' message and why Jesus was born in a stable instead of a palace. I think it's because God loves to use humble things to show His greatness."

SHE GLANCED AT HER notes, then looked back at the class. "The shepherds weren't important people. They didn't have a lot of money or power. But God chose them to be the first ones to hear about Jesus. And the stable wasn't a fancy place—it was just a simple shelter for animals. But God chose it to be the place where the Savior of the world was born."

One of the younger boys raised his hand. "Why didn't God choose something bigger? Like a castle?"

Abby smiled, remembering her own question from the night before. "I think it's because God wants us to know that we don't have to be rich or powerful for Him to use us. It's not about how important we are—it's about how great He is. When He works through humble people and places, it shows everyone that it's His power and His love that make the difference."

THE CLASS SAT QUIETLY for a moment, thinking about her words. Then Miss Clara stepped forward, her eyes bright with encouragement. "That's a beautiful thought, Abby," she said. "The shepherds and the stable remind us that God sees value in things the world often overlooks. He chooses the humble to accomplish great things because their hearts are open to Him."

THAT AFTERNOON, ABBY'S words stayed with her classmates. At home, she decided to put her thoughts into action. She helped her little brother, Ben, clean up his toys, even though she didn't feel like it. She wrote a thank-you note to Miss Clara for being such a kind teacher. And when her mom asked if she'd like to visit the nursing home with her later that week, Abby said yes, knowing it was a way to share God's love with people who might feel forgotten.

Each small act felt like a reflection of the stable—a simple offering that God could use in big ways.

ON CHRISTMAS EVE, AS Abby sat with her family by the tree, she thought about the shepherds again. She thought about how they had gone out into the streets of Bethlehem, telling everyone they could find about the Savior. They didn't have much to give, but they gave their voices, their joy, and their hearts.

Looking at the nativity scene on the mantle, Abby whispered a quiet prayer. "God, thank You for choosing the humble. Help me to be like the shepherds, ready to share Your love and be part of Your plan, no matter how small I feel."

Day 24 - A Family's Obedience

The soft hum of Christmas carols played in the background as the children gathered in the church's fellowship hall for their weekly Sunday school lesson. Snow was falling outside, covering the world in a blanket of white, but inside, the room was warm and filled with the laughter and chatter of excited voices.

Miss Clara, their beloved teacher, stood at the front of the room, holding a large Bible in her hands. She smiled as the children settled into their seats, her kind eyes sparkling with the joy of the season.

"Today, we're going to talk about two very important people in the Christmas story," she began. "Mary and Joseph. Does anyone know what made them so special?"

"They were Jesus' parents!" Ben said, raising his hand eagerly.

"That's right," Miss Clara said. "But do you know what made them stand out? It wasn't that they were rich or famous or powerful. It was their obedience to God. They trusted Him and followed His plan, even when it wasn't easy."

ABBY RAISED HER HAND, her brow furrowed. "Wasn't Mary scared when the angel told her she was going to have a baby? She wasn't even married to Joseph yet."

"That's a great question," Miss Clara said, nodding. "Mary was probably very scared. The Bible tells us that when the angel appeared to her, she was troubled at first. But the angel told her not to be afraid, that she had found favor with God. And even though she didn't understand everything, Mary said, 'Behold the handmaid of the Lord; be it unto me according to thy word.'"

Abby tilted her head, thinking. "So, she trusted God, even though she didn't know how it would all work out?"

"Exactly," Miss Clara said. "Mary showed great faith and obedience. She believed that God's plan was good, even though it was going to change her whole life."

MISS CLARA WALKED OVER to a large poster she had set up at the front of the room. It showed Joseph in a dream, with an angel speaking to him. "Now let's talk about Joseph," she said. "Does anyone remember what happened when he found out Mary was going to have a baby?"

Ben raised his hand again. "He was going to call off their marriage, right?"

"That's right," Miss Clara said. "Joseph was a good man, and he didn't want Mary to be embarrassed or hurt. But he didn't understand yet that the baby she was carrying was from God. Then an angel appeared to him in a dream and said, 'Joseph, son of David, do not be afraid to take Mary as your wife. For the child conceived in her is from the Holy Spirit.'"

The children listened intently as Miss Clara continued. "The angel told Joseph that Mary's baby would save His people from their sins and that he was to name Him Jesus. When Joseph woke up, he did exactly what the angel said. He took Mary as his wife and became the earthly father of the Son of God."

THE ROOM WAS QUIET for a moment as the children absorbed the story. Then Chloe raised her hand. "But wasn't it hard for them? People probably didn't understand what was going on."

"You're absolutely right," Miss Clara said. "It wasn't easy. People might have talked about them behind their backs or doubted their story. And later, they had to travel all the way to Bethlehem, where Mary gave birth in a stable. But through it all, Mary and Joseph obeyed God because they trusted Him."

THE CHILDREN SAT QUIETLY, their minds filled with the images of Mary and Joseph's journey. Abby closed her eyes, imagining Mary riding on a donkey, her face weary but peaceful. Joseph walked beside her, his hand on the reins, his eyes scanning the road ahead. They didn't have a map or a comfortable place to stay, but they carried something greater—faith that God's plan was unfolding, even in the midst of uncertainty.

MISS CLARA'S VOICE broke the silence. "What do you think we can learn from Mary and Joseph's obedience?"

The children exchanged thoughtful glances. Finally, Ben spoke up. "That we should trust God, even when it's hard?"

"Yes," Miss Clara said, smiling. "Obedience isn't always easy. Sometimes it means doing things we don't fully understand or facing challenges we didn't expect. But when we trust God and follow His plan, He can use us to do amazing things—just like He used Mary and Joseph."

LATER THAT AFTERNOON, Abby sat at her desk, her Bible open to the story of Mary and Joseph. She read the verses slowly, her finger tracing the words:

"Then Joseph being raised from sleep did as the angel of the Lord had bidden him, and took unto him his wife." (Matthew 1:24)

She thought about how hard that must have been for Joseph, to trust a dream and step into a situation he didn't fully understand. And Mary—how brave she had been to say yes to God's plan, even though it meant her life would never be the same.

ABBY PICKED UP HER journal and began to write:

"Mary and Joseph remind me that obedience to God isn't always easy, but it's always worth it. They didn't know how everything would work out, but they trusted God anyway. I want to have that kind of faith."

As she wrote, she thought about the times she found it hard to obey—like when her mom asked her to clean her room when she wanted to play outside, or when she had to be kind to a classmate who wasn't always nice to her. Those things seemed small compared to what Mary and Joseph had done, but Abby realized that even small acts of obedience could show her trust in God.

THE NEXT MORNING, ABBY decided to put what she had learned into practice. When her little brother Ben asked her to play a game with him, even though she had been planning to read a book, she said yes. Later, when her mom asked her to help set the table for dinner, she did it without complaining. Each small act felt like a step of faith, a way of saying, "I trust You, God."

ON CHRISTMAS EVE, AS Abby sat with her family in church, the sanctuary glowing with candlelight, she thought about Mary and Joseph again. She thought about how their obedience had made it possible for the Savior to come into the world. And she realized that their story wasn't just something to admire—it was something to follow.

As the congregation sang "O Holy Night," Abby whispered a quiet prayer. "Thank You, God, for Mary and Joseph's example. Help me to trust You and follow Your plan, even when it's hard."

Day 25 - The Role of Angels

The warm light of the Christmas tree filled the living room as Chloe curled up on the couch with her favorite blanket. Her little brother, Ben, sat cross-legged on the floor, sorting through the colorful angel ornaments they were about to hang on the tree. Each one was unique—some made of glass, others crafted from wood or delicate paper. Chloe's dad sat in his armchair, his Bible resting on his lap, and smiled as he watched them.

"Dad," Chloe said, holding up a delicate angel ornament with golden wings, "why are angels such a big part of the Christmas story? They're everywhere—in songs, decorations, and even the nativity play we're doing at church."

Her dad leaned forward, his eyes warm and thoughtful. "That's a great question, Chloe. Angels play an important role in the Christmas story because they were messengers. God used them to communicate His plan and to bring amazing news to the people involved."

Ben looked up, holding a glittery angel in his hands. "Like when the angel told Mary she was going to have Jesus?"

"Exactly," Dad said, nodding. "The angel Gabriel was sent to Mary to tell her something incredible—that she had been chosen by God to be the mother of the Savior. And that wasn't the only time angels showed up in the story."

Chloe tilted her head, intrigued. "What else did they do?"

HER DAD OPENED HIS Bible to the book of Luke, turning to the first chapter. "Let's start with Mary," he said, his voice steady and gentle. "The Bible says that God sent the angel Gabriel to a town called Nazareth, to a young woman named Mary. Gabriel appeared to her and said, 'Hail, thou that art highly favoured, the Lord is with thee: blessed art thou among women.'"

Chloe closed her eyes, picturing the scene. She imagined Mary, perhaps in the middle of her daily chores, suddenly seeing a bright and glorious figure standing before her. The angel's presence must have been overwhelming—his face radiant, his voice calm but powerful.

Her dad continued reading. "The Bible says Mary was troubled at the angel's words and wondered what kind of greeting this could be. But Gabriel said, 'Fear not, Mary: for thou hast found favour with God. And, behold, thou shalt conceive in thy womb, and bring forth a son, and shalt call his name Jesus.'"

Ben's eyes widened. "I'd be scared if an angel just showed up like that."

Chloe laughed. "Me too. But Mary wasn't scared for long, right, Dad?"

"Right," her dad said. "Mary listened to the angel and trusted what he said. Even though she didn't understand how it would happen, she said, 'Behold the handmaid of the Lord; be it unto me according to thy word.' She showed incredible faith and obedience."

CHLOE IMAGINED MARY'S heart pounding as she heard Gabriel's message. She pictured the angel's glowing wings and the gentle reassurance in his voice as he explained God's plan. Mary's courage and willingness to trust God filled Chloe with admiration.

"But Gabriel didn't just visit Mary," Dad said, flipping a few pages in his Bible. "He also appeared to someone else—Mary's cousin Elizabeth's husband, Zacharias. He told Zacharias that he and Elizabeth, even though they were old, would have a son named John, who would prepare the way for Jesus."

Ben's mouth fell open. "An angel told him too? That's so cool."

"It is," Dad agreed. "And later, an angel appeared to Joseph in a dream. Joseph was worried when he found out Mary was going to have a baby, but the angel told him, 'Fear not to take unto thee Mary thy wife: for that which is conceived in her is of the Holy Ghost.'"

CHLOE THOUGHT ABOUT Joseph, waking up from his dream and realizing that the angel's message had changed everything. She imagined him looking at Mary with new understanding and deciding to trust God's plan, even though it must have been hard.

"But the angels didn't stop there," Dad said, his voice filled with excitement. "After Jesus was born, angels appeared to the shepherds out in the fields. They brought the best news anyone could ever hear: 'For unto you is born this day in the city of David a Saviour, which is Christ the Lord.'"

Ben grinned. "I remember that part! The angel told them to go find baby Jesus, and then a whole bunch of angels showed up, singing."

"Exactly," Dad said. "The sky was filled with a multitude of the heavenly host, praising God and saying, 'Glory to God in the highest, and on earth peace, good will toward men.' Can you imagine what that must have looked like?"

IN CHLOE'S MIND, THE hills outside Bethlehem came alive. She pictured the shepherds staring up in awe as the night sky blazed with light and the sound of angelic voices filled the air. The message of peace and joy was so powerful that the shepherds immediately left their flocks to find Jesus.

"So, angels were like God's messengers," Chloe said, her voice thoughtful. "They brought news, gave instructions, and helped people trust God's plan."

Her dad nodded. "That's right. Angels show us that God communicates in amazing ways. Sometimes it's through angels, but other times it's through His Word, through other people, or even through the quiet thoughts and feelings in our hearts. The important thing is to listen and be ready to respond, just like Mary, Joseph, and the shepherds did."

THAT EVENING, AFTER the ornaments were hung and the tree was aglow with lights, Chloe sat by the fire with her journal. She opened to a blank page and wrote at the top: "What I Can Learn from the Angels."

She thought about Gabriel's visit to Mary, the angel's message to Joseph, and the host of angels proclaiming Jesus' birth to the shepherds. Each moment was filled with purpose, with God using His messengers to share His plan of love and salvation.

Chloe began to write:

- Angels remind us to trust God's messages, even when they're surprising.

- Angels brought joy and peace by sharing the good news. I can do that too.

- God's plan is bigger than we can see, but He always makes sure we know what we need to do.

THE NEXT MORNING, CHLOE decided to share what she had learned. When her family gathered for breakfast, she read from her journal, explaining how the angels in the Christmas story had inspired her. Her mom and dad listened with proud smiles, and Ben chimed in with his favorite part about the angels singing to the shepherds.

Later, Chloe looked for ways to bring the angels' message of peace and joy into her own life. She helped her neighbor carry groceries up the icy steps to her porch, surprising the older woman with her kindness. She wrote a note of encouragement for her teacher, who had been looking tired lately. Each act felt like a way of reflecting the light and hope the angels had shared so long ago.

ON CHRISTMAS EVE, AS Chloe stood with her family in church, holding a flickering candle during the final hymn, she felt a quiet joy in her heart. She thought about the angels, their voices ringing out across the hills of Bethlehem, and she whispered a prayer.

"Thank You, God, for sending angels to share the good news of Jesus. Help me to be like them—sharing Your love and joy with everyone I meet."

Day 26 - God's Perfect Timing

The snow fell softly outside the living room window, blanketing the world in quiet stillness. Ben sat on the couch, his legs tucked under him, staring at the glowing Christmas tree. The house was peaceful, with the faint hum of Christmas music drifting from the kitchen where his mom was finishing the dishes. Ben held his Bible in his lap, open to a verse he had read earlier in Sunday school:

"But when the fulness of the time was come, God sent forth his Son, made of a woman, made under the law." (Galatians 4:4)

He read the words again, letting them sink in. "The fulness of the time." It sounded important, but Ben wasn't sure what it really meant. Why had Jesus come when He did? Why not sooner—or later?

BEN TURNED AS HIS DAD walked into the room, carrying a cup of tea. He sat down in the armchair near the tree, his eyes crinkling with a smile. "You look deep in thought," his dad said. "What's on your mind?"

Ben pointed to the verse in his Bible. "We talked about this in Sunday school today," he said. "It says Jesus came when the time was just right. Why was it the right time? What made it perfect?"

His dad took a sip of tea, setting the mug on the side table. "That's a great question, Ben," he said. "The Bible tells us that God's timing is always perfect, even if we don't understand it right away. Jesus came into the world at exactly the right moment—not just for the people back then, but for all of us."

BEN TILTED HIS HEAD, intrigued. "But how did God decide it was the right time? What made it so special?"

His dad leaned back, his expression thoughtful. "Let's think about it together. Back then, the world was under Roman rule. The Roman Empire had built roads that connected cities and countries like never before, making it easier for people to travel and share news. And there was a common language, Greek, that most people understood. It was the perfect setup for the good news of Jesus to spread quickly."

Ben nodded slowly, trying to picture it. "So, it was like God had been preparing the world?"

"Exactly," his dad said. "And it wasn't just about the roads or the language. God's people, the Israelites, had been waiting for a Savior for hundreds of years. They had read the prophecies and prayed for the Messiah to come. When Jesus was born, it fulfilled those promises. It was the moment they had been hoping for, even if it didn't look the way they expected."

BEN'S MIND FILLED WITH images of the Christmas story. He thought about Mary and Joseph, traveling to Bethlehem because of the Roman census. He imagined the shepherds, their quiet night on the hills interrupted by the angel's announcement. He pictured the wise men, journeying across deserts to follow the star. Every piece of the story seemed to fit together perfectly, like the pieces of a puzzle.

"So, God had it all planned out?" Ben asked.

"Yes," his dad said. "God's plan was in motion long before Jesus was born. Even when it seemed like nothing was happening, He was preparing the way. And when the time was just right, Jesus came."

BEN THOUGHT ABOUT THE long wait the Israelites had endured, their hope stretching across generations. He tried to imagine what it must have been like for them, holding on to God's promises even when they didn't see them come true right away.

"It must have been hard to wait," he said softly. "What if they got tired of waiting?"

"I'm sure some of them did," his dad said. "But God's faithfulness never wavered, even when people doubted or lost hope. And when Jesus came, it wasn't just for them—it was for everyone, for all time. That's why His birth is such an amazing reminder of God's perfect timing."

THE ROOM GREW QUIET as Ben stared at the twinkling lights on the tree. He thought about times when he had prayed for something but hadn't gotten an answer right away. He remembered feeling frustrated, wondering if God was even listening. But this story reminded him that God's plans were always bigger than he could see.

"Dad," he said after a moment, "do you think God's timing is still perfect today?"

His dad smiled. "Absolutely, Ben. God's timing hasn't changed. Sometimes we don't understand why things happen the way they do, or why we have to wait. But when we trust Him, we can know that He's working everything out for good."

LATER THAT NIGHT, AS Ben got ready for bed, he found himself thinking about the verse again. "The fulness of the time." He thought about how God had orchestrated every detail of Jesus' birth, from the Roman census that brought Mary and Joseph to Bethlehem to the star that guided the wise men. It made him realize that even when things seemed random or confusing, God was always in control.

Before climbing into bed, Ben opened his journal and wrote at the top of a blank page: What I've Learned About God's Timing. He began to list the thoughts that had been swirling in his mind:

- God's timing is always perfect, even when we don't see it.
- Jesus came at the right time to save us and bring us closer to God.
- Sometimes waiting is part of God's plan, and that's okay.

He paused, tapping the pen against his chin, then added one more line: Trust God's plan—it's worth the wait.

THE NEXT DAY, BEN DECIDED to share what he had learned with his little sister, Emma. As they built a snowman in the backyard, he told her about how God had planned Jesus' birth to happen at the perfect time.

"Does that mean God plans everything?" Emma asked, packing snow into a ball.

"Pretty much," Ben said. "Even when it feels like nothing's happening, He's working on something good. It's like building this snowman. We have to do it one step at a time, and it doesn't look like much at first. But when we're done, it's exactly how it's supposed to be."

Emma grinned. "So, God's plan is like a snowman?"

Ben laughed. "Kind of! But way bigger and way better."

THAT EVENING, AS BEN sat with his family by the fire, he thought about how Jesus' birth had changed everything. He thought about how God's timing wasn't just perfect back then—it was perfect now, too. And as he stared at the glowing embers in the fireplace, he whispered a prayer in his heart.

"Thank You, God, for sending Jesus at the perfect time. Help me to trust Your timing in my life, even when it's hard to wait."

Day 27 - A King Born in a Manger

The classroom buzzed with the quiet excitement of children finishing their paper crowns. Golden-colored paper, glitter, and glue sticks were scattered across the tables as each child carefully decorated their crown to look as royal as possible. Chloe adjusted her crown, admiring the shiny red gem sticker she had placed in the center. Beside her, Ben was painstakingly gluing silver sequins onto the tips of his crown.

Miss Clara, their Sunday school teacher, stood at the front of the room, her hands folded over her Bible. "Those are some beautiful crowns you're making," she said with a warm smile. "You all look like real royalty!"

The children beamed, straightening their crowns and sitting a little taller. "Today," Miss Clara continued, "we're going to talk about a King—one unlike any other. He didn't wear a fancy crown or sit on a golden throne. Do you know who I'm talking about?"

"Jesus!" several children said in unison.

"That's right," Miss Clara said. "Jesus is the King of Kings, but His life started in a very different way than most kings. Let's talk about why."

THE CHILDREN LEANED forward as Miss Clara began. "When we think of kings, what usually comes to mind? What do kings have?"

"Castles!" Chloe said, raising her hand.

"Gold and treasure," Ben added.

"Fancy clothes and servants!" another boy chimed in.

Miss Clara nodded. "Exactly. Kings are usually surrounded by wealth, power, and luxury. But when Jesus, the King of Kings, came into the world, He wasn't born in a palace. He didn't have riches or servants. Instead, He was born in a humble stable, and His first bed was a manger—a feeding trough for animals."

CHLOE'S EYES WIDENED. "A manger? That doesn't sound very kingly."

"It doesn't, does it?" Miss Clara said, smiling. "But Jesus' birth shows us something very important about what it means to be truly great. Jesus didn't come to be served, but to serve. He came to show us that true greatness isn't about power or riches—it's about love, humility, and helping others."

Miss Clara picked up her Bible and turned to Mark 10:45. "Let's listen to what Jesus said about why He came: 'For even the Son of man came not to be ministered unto, but to minister, and to give His life a ransom for many.'"

AS MISS CLARA SPOKE, Chloe's mind filled with images of the nativity story. She imagined Mary and Joseph arriving in Bethlehem, tired from their long journey, only to find that every inn was full. She pictured the small stable where they finally found shelter, the rough wooden manger filled with hay, and the animals quietly resting nearby. And in the midst of it all, baby Jesus—God's Son, born not into splendor but into simplicity.

MISS CLARA CONTINUED, her voice calm but filled with passion. "Jesus' humble birth was a message to the whole world. It showed that God's love is for everyone—not just for the rich or powerful, but for the poor, the ordinary, and the overlooked. By being born in a manger, Jesus taught us that greatness comes from serving others and putting their needs before our own."

Ben raised his hand, his brow furrowed. "But why would Jesus want to be born like that? He could have had a palace if He wanted."

Miss Clara smiled, nodding at Ben's question. "Jesus could have had anything He wanted. But He chose humility to show us what God's kingdom is like. In God's kingdom, the greatest are those who serve. Jesus lived that out from the moment He was born to the day He gave His life on the cross."

THE CHILDREN SAT QUIETLY, their paper crowns forgotten for the moment as they thought about Miss Clara's words. Chloe spoke up, her voice soft. "So, Jesus wasn't just a King. He was a servant too?"

"That's right," Miss Clara said. "Jesus showed us that being a servant is the greatest way to lead. He cared for the sick, welcomed the outcasts, and even washed His disciples' feet. And the greatest act of all was when He gave His life for us so that we could be forgiven and have a relationship with God."

AFTER THE LESSON, MISS Clara handed each child a small card with the words "But he that is greatest among you shall be your servant." (Matthew 23:11) written in elegant script. "I want you to think about ways you can follow Jesus' example of serving others," she said. "It doesn't have to be something big—even small acts of kindness can make a difference."

Chloe stared at her card, her mind racing with ideas. She thought about her little brother, who always wanted her to play with him but often heard "not now" or "maybe later." She thought about her elderly neighbor, Mrs. Carter, who lived alone and always seemed so happy when Chloe stopped by to say hello. Serving didn't seem so hard when she thought about it that way—it was just about loving people the way Jesus did.

THAT AFTERNOON, CHLOE put her plan into action. When her brother Ben asked her to build a block tower with him, she said yes, even though she had been planning to draw in her sketchbook. Later, she helped her mom bake cookies and delivered a plate of them to Mrs. Carter, who smiled so brightly that Chloe's heart felt warm all over.

As she walked home, Chloe thought about the stable again. She realized that Jesus' birth in such a humble place wasn't just part of the story—it was the heart of the story. It showed that greatness wasn't about being served, but about serving others with love and kindness.

THAT EVENING, AS CHLOE sat by the fire with her family, she told them about what she had learned. "Jesus could have been born in a palace," she said, "but He chose a manger because He wanted to show us that true greatness is about serving. I want to be like that too."

Her dad smiled, reaching over to ruffle her hair. "That's a beautiful way to live, Chloe. The world needs more people who follow Jesus' example."

ON CHRISTMAS EVE, AS Chloe stood with her family in church, holding a flickering candle during the final hymn, she whispered a quiet prayer. "Thank You, Jesus, for being a King who serves. Help me to follow Your example and show Your love to others."

Day 28 - Joy to the World

The church sanctuary was alive with the sounds of children's laughter and excited whispers as they gathered on the stage for their Christmas program rehearsal. Abby stood in the front row, her red sweater bright against the dark wood of the choir risers. Next to her, Chloe adjusted her Santa hat, her cheeks flushed with excitement. Ben was in the back row, whispering jokes to Jonah until Miss Clara, their Sunday school teacher, shot him a playful but firm look.

"Okay, everyone," Miss Clara said, clapping her hands to get their attention. "This is the big finale of the program—'Joy to the World.' We've practiced the verses and the chorus, but today I want us to really think about what this song means."

The children exchanged curious glances. It was just a song, wasn't it? They had sung it a hundred times before, their voices rising and falling with the familiar melody. But Miss Clara had a way of turning even the most ordinary things into something special.

MISS CLARA STEPPED closer, her smile warm and inviting. "Before we sing, let's talk about joy. What is joy, and why do you think it's such a big part of the Christmas story?"

"Is it like being happy?" Chloe asked, tilting her head.

"Yes, it's like happiness," Miss Clara said, "but it's even deeper. Joy is something we feel when we know how much God loves us and that He's with us, no matter what. It's a kind of happiness that doesn't go away, even when things are hard."

Abby raised her hand. "Is that why the angels said 'good tidings of great joy' to the shepherds?"

"Exactly!" Miss Clara said, her eyes lighting up. "Let's read that part of the story together."

MISS CLARA OPENED HER Bible to Luke 2:10 and began to read: "And the angel said unto them, Fear not: for, behold, I bring you good tidings of great joy, which shall be to all people."

She looked up, her voice softening. "The angel wasn't just bringing news of a baby being born. He was announcing the arrival of the Savior—the One who would bring peace, hope, and joy to the whole world. That's why we sing 'Joy to the World.' It's a celebration of what Jesus' birth means for everyone."

THE CHILDREN GREW QUIET, the weight of her words sinking in. Abby thought about the shepherds on that quiet hillside, their ordinary night suddenly transformed by the brilliance of angels filling the sky. She imagined their fear turning to awe, their hearts filling with a joy so overwhelming they couldn't help but run to Bethlehem to see the baby for themselves.

"So, when we sing this song," Miss Clara continued, "we're joining with the angels and the shepherds in proclaiming the joy that Jesus brings. And the best part? That joy isn't just for the people who were there that night—it's for all of us, too."

MISS CLARA MOTIONED for the pianist to begin, and the familiar notes of "Joy to the World" filled the sanctuary. The children stood a little straighter, their voices rising together in the first verse:

"Joy to the world, the Lord is come!

Let earth receive her King;

Let every heart prepare Him room,

And heaven and nature sing..."

Abby felt a thrill as she sang, her voice blending with those of her friends. She thought about the words, about how the whole world was invited to rejoice because Jesus had come. The image of angels and shepherds celebrating filled her mind, and for a moment, she felt like she was part of that scene, joining in their song of praise.

AFTER THEY FINISHED the song, Miss Clara clapped her hands. "That was beautiful! But before we go, I want you to think about something. How can we share the joy of Jesus' birth with others?"

Ben raised his hand, his face thoughtful. "By telling them about Jesus?"

"Yes," Miss Clara said, nodding. "Sharing the good news is one way. But there are other ways too. Can you think of anything else?"

Chloe's hand shot up. "By being kind to people, even if they're not kind to us?"

"Absolutely," Miss Clara said. "When we show love, kindness, and forgiveness, we're sharing the joy of Jesus with the world. And what about helping someone who's feeling sad or lonely? That's another way to bring joy."

THE CHILDREN BEGAN to brainstorm, their ideas coming quickly now. They talked about writing cards to elderly neighbors, making cookies for friends, and including new kids at school. Each idea felt like a little spark of light, a way to reflect the joy they had been singing about.

THAT EVENING, AS ABBY sat by the fire at home, she thought about what Miss Clara had said. Joy wasn't just a feeling—it was something you could share. She decided to start small. She wrote a note for her mom, thanking her for all the ways she made Christmas special. Then she helped her little brother wrap a present for their dad, even though she'd much rather be reading her book.

As she worked, Abby felt the kind of happiness that Miss Clara had described—not the fleeting kind, but a deep, steady joy that came from knowing Jesus and sharing His love.

THE NEXT DAY, DURING the final dress rehearsal, the children sang "Joy to the World" again, their voices ringing out with new energy. Abby noticed how everyone seemed more connected, their hearts full of the meaning behind the words.

After the rehearsal, Chloe pulled Abby aside. "I was thinking about what Miss Clara said," she whispered. "About sharing joy. Do you think we could visit Mrs. Carter after the program tomorrow? She's always alone, and I think she'd like to hear the song."

Abby's face lit up. "That's a great idea! We could bring her some cookies too."

ON CHRISTMAS EVE, AFTER the program ended and the congregation's applause echoed through the sanctuary, Chloe and Abby carried their plan into action. With a tin of cookies in hand, they walked to Mrs. Carter's house and knocked on the door. When the elderly woman opened it, her face lit up with surprise.

"Merry Christmas!" Abby said, holding out the cookies. "We thought you might like some company."

"And a song," Chloe added with a grin.

The girls sang "Joy to the World" right there on the porch, their voices clear and joyful in the crisp night air. Mrs. Carter's eyes filled with tears as she listened, and when the song ended, she pulled them both into a warm hug.

"You've made my Christmas so special," she said, her voice trembling. "Thank you."

AS ABBY AND CHLOE WALKED home, their hearts felt as bright as the stars above them. They realized that sharing the joy of Jesus wasn't about doing something big or impressive—it was about showing love in simple, heartfelt ways.

That night, as Abby knelt by her bed to pray, she whispered, "Thank You, Jesus, for bringing joy to the world. Help me to share that joy with everyone I meet."

Day 29 - The Name Above All Names

The quiet of the winter evening wrapped around the small church as families gathered inside for the children's Christmas Bible study. The warm glow of candlelight flickered against the stained-glass windows, casting colorful patterns on the walls. Abby sat near the front of the room with her Bible open in her lap, her fingers tracing the edges of the pages. She had always loved Christmas, but tonight she felt a special excitement. Miss Clara had promised to talk about something "very important" that had to do with Jesus.

Miss Clara stood at the front, her kind smile glowing as she held up her Bible. "Tonight, we're going to talk about a name—a name so important, so powerful, that it changes everything. Can anyone guess what it is?"

"Jesus!" Ben shouted from the second row, his enthusiasm drawing giggles from the other children.

"That's right," Miss Clara said, nodding. "The name of Jesus. But what makes His name so special? Why is it called the name above all names?"

The room grew quiet as the children pondered her question. Abby raised her hand, her voice soft but clear. "Is it because He's the Savior?"

Miss Clara's smile widened. "Exactly, Abby. Let's look at what the Bible says about the name of Jesus. Turn to Philippians 2:9-10."

ABBY FLIPPED THROUGH her Bible, finding the verse. As Miss Clara read aloud, Abby followed along:

"Wherefore God also hath highly exalted Him, and given Him a name which is above every name: That at the name of Jesus every knee should bow, of things in heaven, and things in earth, and things under the earth."

Miss Clara paused, letting the words sink in. "This verse tells us that Jesus' name is the most powerful, most important name there is. It's a name that brings hope, healing, and salvation. But to understand why, we need to go back to the beginning—to the Christmas story."

AS MISS CLARA BEGAN to recount the story of Jesus' birth, Abby's mind filled with familiar images. She pictured Mary and Joseph traveling to Bethlehem, the crowded inns, and the quiet stable where Jesus was born. She thought about the angel who appeared to Joseph in a dream, telling him to name the baby Jesus, because He would save His people from their sins.

"Does anyone know what the name 'Jesus' means?" Miss Clara asked, her eyes scanning the room.

Abby's hand shot up. "It means 'God saves,' right?"

"Exactly," Miss Clara said. "The name Jesus comes from the Hebrew name Yeshua, which means 'The Lord is salvation.' From the moment He was born, Jesus was given a name that showed His purpose. He came to save us from our sins and to bring us back into a relationship with God."

AS MISS CLARA SPOKE, Abby thought about the power of that name. She imagined the shepherds kneeling before the manger, whispering the name of Jesus as they gazed at the tiny baby. She pictured the wise men, their voices filled with reverence as they offered their gifts. Even as a baby, Jesus carried a name that would change the world.

"But Jesus' name isn't just powerful because of what it means," Miss Clara continued. "It's powerful because of what He did. Jesus lived a perfect life, showed us how to love and serve others, and then gave His life on the cross to save us. When we call on His name, we're trusting in everything He has done for us."

BEN RAISED HIS HAND, his brow furrowed in thought. "So, when we pray and say 'in Jesus' name,' does that mean we're asking for His help?"

"Yes, Ben," Miss Clara said. "When we pray in Jesus' name, we're recognizing that He is our Savior and that His power is at work in our lives. The name of Jesus reminds us that we can trust Him with everything—our fears, our hopes, and our needs."

LATER THAT EVENING, after the study ended and the children returned home, Abby sat by the Christmas tree with her journal. She opened to a blank page and wrote at the top: What the Name of Jesus Means to Me.

She thought about the times she had whispered His name in prayer—when she was scared of a storm, when she felt nervous about a test, or when she simply wanted to thank Him for something good. Each time, she had felt a sense of peace, as if Jesus Himself was right there with her.

Abby began to write:

- The name of Jesus means God is always with me.

- It reminds me that He loves me and saves me.

- When I say His name, I know I can trust Him.

THE NEXT MORNING, ABBY decided to share what she had learned with her little brother, Ben. As they sat at the kitchen table eating breakfast, she told him about the meaning of Jesus' name and why it was so important.

"Did you know that every time we say 'Jesus,' we're saying 'God saves'?" she asked.

Ben's eyes widened. "Really? That's cool."

Abby nodded. "And when we pray in His name, we're asking Him to help us, just like Miss Clara said. It's like having a direct connection to God."

Ben grinned. "That's like having a superhero's name to call out for help!"

Abby laughed. "Kind of, but even better. Jesus isn't just a superhero—He's our Savior."

THAT AFTERNOON, AS Abby and Ben helped their mom deliver cookies to their neighbors, Abby thought about how she could share the name of Jesus with others. When they reached Mrs. Thompson's house, Abby handed her a plate of cookies and said, "Merry Christmas! We made these to remind you how much God loves you. That's why He sent Jesus."

Mrs. Thompson's eyes filled with tears as she accepted the gift. "Thank you, Abby," she said. "That's a beautiful reminder."

As they walked to the next house, Abby felt a warmth in her heart. Sharing the name of Jesus wasn't just about saying it—it was about showing His love through her actions.

ON CHRISTMAS EVE, AS Abby stood with her family in the candlelit sanctuary, the congregation began to sing "What a Beautiful Name." Abby's voice rose with the others, her heart full as she thought about the name of Jesus and all it meant. She pictured the shepherds and the wise men again, their voices joining with the angels in praising the One who had come to save.

As the song ended, Abby bowed her head and whispered a prayer. "Thank You, Jesus, for Your name and everything it means. Help me to always remember how powerful and loving You are."

Day 30 - Sharing the Christmas Story

The crisp December air filled the small church hall as the children gathered for their final Sunday school class before Christmas. Snowflakes swirled outside the frosted windows, and the faint scent of pine and cinnamon lingered in the air. Daniel sat near the front, his Bible open on his lap, listening as Miss Clara shared the last part of their lesson for the day.

"Christmas is such a special time," Miss Clara said, her voice warm and full of energy. "It's a time to celebrate Jesus' birth, to remember why He came, and—just as importantly—to share that good news with others. Does anyone know what Jesus told His disciples after He rose from the dead?"

Daniel raised his hand eagerly. "He said to go and tell everyone about Him!"

"That's right," Miss Clara said, nodding. "In Matthew 28:19-20, Jesus gave us what's called the Great Commission. He said, 'Go ye therefore, and teach all nations, baptizing them in the name of the Father, and of the Son, and of the Holy Ghost: Teaching them to observe all things whatsoever I have commanded you.' Jesus wants everyone to know about His love and salvation. And that's something we can do, too."

AS MISS CLARA'S WORDS sank in, Daniel felt a spark of excitement. He loved the Christmas story—the angel's announcement, the journey to Bethlehem, the baby in the manger, and the shepherds and wise men worshiping Jesus. But he had never thought about how important it was to share that story with others.

After class, as the children gathered their things and prepared to leave, Daniel approached Miss Clara. "Miss Clara," he began, his voice hesitant but hopeful, "I have an idea."

She smiled warmly. "What is it, Daniel?"

"Well," he said, shifting on his feet, "what if we acted out the Christmas story for the Christmas Eve service? We could invite people from the neighborhood to come and watch, even if they don't usually go to church. It would be a way to share the story with them."

MISS CLARA'S FACE LIT up. "Daniel, that's a wonderful idea! The Christmas story is the greatest news anyone can hear, and sharing it through a play could be a beautiful way to invite others to learn about Jesus. Let's talk to Pastor John and see if we can make it happen."

By the time Daniel left the church that morning, he could hardly contain his excitement. He told his parents about the idea on the way home, and they both smiled with pride. "What a great way to share the meaning of Christmas," his mom said. "We're proud of you, Daniel."

THE FOLLOWING WEEK was a whirlwind of activity. Miss Clara and Pastor John helped the children plan the play, assigning roles and organizing rehearsals. Daniel was chosen to narrate the story, reading directly from the Bible, while his friends took on the roles of Mary, Joseph, the shepherds, the wise men, and even the angels. Chloe offered to help with costumes, gathering simple robes and headscarves for the cast. Abby worked with Miss Clara to create props, including a wooden manger and a shining star to hang above the stage.

As they rehearsed, the children grew more excited. Each scene came to life as they practiced their lines and movements, their laughter filling the hall as they worked together. Daniel felt a sense of purpose he had never experienced before. This wasn't just a fun activity—it was a way to share the most important story in the world.

ON CHRISTMAS EVE, THE sanctuary was filled with people. Families from the church and neighbors from the community packed the pews, their faces glowing in the soft light of the candles and twinkling decorations. Daniel peeked out from behind the curtain, his heart pounding with a mix of nerves and excitement.

"Ready?" Miss Clara whispered, placing a reassuring hand on his shoulder.

Daniel nodded. "I'm ready."

The lights dimmed, and Pastor John stepped forward to welcome everyone. "Tonight, our children have prepared a special presentation of the Christmas story," he said. "It's a story of hope, love, and salvation—a story that reminds us of the greatest gift ever given. Let's open our hearts and celebrate together."

AS THE PLAY BEGAN, Daniel's voice filled the sanctuary, steady and clear as he narrated the opening lines from Luke 2:1-7. "And it came to pass in those days, that there went out a decree from Caesar Augustus, that all the world should be taxed..."

Mary and Joseph, played by Chloe and Ben, walked slowly across the stage, their costumes simple but effective. The children in the audience watched with wide eyes as the story unfolded—the innkeeper shaking his head, the humble stable, and the manger prepared for the newborn King.

When the angel appeared to the shepherds, played by a group of younger children, Daniel read the angel's words with conviction: "Fear not: for, behold, I bring you good tidings of great joy, which shall be to all people. For unto you is born this day in the city of David a Saviour, which is Christ the Lord."

AS THE SHEPHERDS RAN to the manger, their excitement genuine even in their pretend roles, Daniel felt a swell of joy. He could see the faces of the audience members, many of whom looked deeply moved. Some wiped away tears as the children acted out the wise men's journey, kneeling before the manger with their gifts of gold, frankincense, and myrrh.

The final scene brought the entire cast to the stage, gathered around the manger as Daniel read the closing verses. "And the shepherds returned, glorifying and praising God for all the things that they had heard and seen, as it was told unto them."

The children began to sing "Silent Night," their voices sweet and clear. The congregation joined in, their voices rising together in a moment of unity and reverence.

AFTER THE PLAY ENDED, the applause was thunderous. Daniel felt a mix of relief and pride as he stood with the other children, bowing before the crowd. But more than anything, he felt grateful—grateful for the chance to share the Christmas story and to remind everyone why they celebrated this special night.

As the audience mingled afterward, Daniel noticed a family he didn't recognize standing near the refreshments table. He approached them hesitantly, his heart pounding.

"Hi," he said. "I'm Daniel. Did you like the play?"

The mother of the family smiled warmly. "We loved it. Thank you for sharing such a beautiful story. We don't usually come to church, but tonight felt special."

Daniel's heart swelled. "I'm glad you came," he said. "Christmas is about Jesus, and we wanted to share His story with everyone."

THAT NIGHT, AS DANIEL lay in bed, he thought about the Great Commission and how Jesus had told His disciples to share the good news with the world. He realized that they had done just that—right here in their little church. It wasn't about being perfect or fancy; it was about sharing the truth of God's love.

Before drifting off to sleep, Daniel whispered a quiet prayer. "Thank You, Jesus, for letting us share Your story. Help me to keep sharing it, not just at Christmas, but every day."

Day 31 - Jesus, the Greatest Gift

The first light of Christmas morning peeked through the frost-covered windows of the Parker household. Abby sat up in her bed, the cozy warmth of her blanket wrapped around her. The faint smell of cinnamon rolls baking in the oven wafted through the air, and she could hear the soft murmurs of her parents talking downstairs. It was Christmas morning—a day she had been eagerly waiting for—but this year, something felt different.

Instead of rushing to her stocking like she usually did, Abby reached for her Bible on her nightstand. She flipped to a verse they had talked about in Sunday school earlier that week: "Thanks be unto God for His unspeakable gift." (2 Corinthians 9:15)

The verse had stuck with her, the idea of Jesus being the greatest gift overshadowing all the excitement about presents and cookies. She wanted to understand it better, to feel the truth of it in her heart.

DOWNSTAIRS, THE HOUSE was coming alive. Ben, her younger brother, was already bouncing around in his pajamas, shouting about the presents under the tree. Chloe, their neighbor and best friend, had spent the night for their annual Christmas Eve sleepover and was helping Abby's mom in the kitchen.

"Abby, come on!" Ben yelled up the stairs. "Santa came! There's so much stuff!"

Abby laughed, slipping out of bed and hurrying downstairs. The living room was a picture of Christmas magic: the tree sparkled with ornaments and lights, and neatly wrapped presents in colorful paper were piled high. But as much as Abby loved the sight, her heart felt drawn to something deeper.

AFTER BREAKFAST, HER dad gathered the family around the tree. He held a small, wrapped gift in his hands and sat on the couch, his face thoughtful. "Before we start opening presents," he said, "I want us to take a moment to think about the greatest gift we've ever received."

Ben's eyes lit up. "Is it already under the tree?"

Her dad chuckled. "Not quite. It's the gift of Jesus. God sent His Son to save us, and that's a gift no amount of money could ever buy."

He unwrapped the small gift in his hands, revealing a simple wooden cross. "This," he said, holding it up, "is a reminder of why we celebrate Christmas. Jesus came into the world as a baby, but He didn't stay a baby. He grew up, lived a perfect life, and gave His life for us. That's what makes Him the greatest gift."

ABBY STARED AT THE cross, her heart swelling with a mixture of gratitude and awe. She thought about the Christmas story—the angel's message to Mary, the humble stable in Bethlehem, and the shepherds kneeling before the manger. It all pointed to one truth: Jesus was God's gift to the world, a gift of love, hope, and salvation.

Her dad passed the cross to her. "What does this gift mean to you, Abby?"

Abby held the cross carefully, her fingers tracing the smooth wood. "It means... God loves us so much that He gave us Jesus," she said slowly. "And because of Jesus, we can be close to God."

"That's exactly right," her dad said, smiling.

BEN FIDGETED NEXT TO her, his eyes darting to the presents under the tree. "But why did God give us Jesus?" he asked. "Why didn't He just fix everything Himself?"

Abby's mom leaned forward, her voice gentle. "God gave us Jesus because He wanted us to know Him in a personal way. Jesus is God with us—He came to live among us, to show us how much God loves us, and to save us from our sins. It's like the verse we've talked about before: 'For God so loved the world, that He gave His only begotten Son.' Jesus is the proof of God's love."

AS THEY PASSED THE cross around the circle, each family member shared what the gift of Jesus meant to them. Chloe spoke about how Jesus gave her peace when she was scared. Ben said Jesus was like a friend who was always there. Abby's mom shared how Jesus had guided her through hard times, and her dad talked about the joy that came from knowing Jesus as Savior.

The room felt quiet and holy, the kind of stillness that made Abby think of the stable in Bethlehem. For a moment, the presents under the tree didn't matter. What mattered was the gift they already had—the greatest gift of all.

AFTER THEY FINISHED, her dad said, "Now, let's make today about sharing this gift. When we open our presents, let's remember that we're celebrating because of Jesus. And let's think about ways we can share His love with others."

AS THE MORNING WENT on, the family opened their gifts, laughter and joy filling the room. But Abby couldn't stop thinking about her dad's words. She looked at the bracelet Chloe had given her, its charm engraved with the word hope, and thought about how Jesus had brought hope to the whole world. She watched Ben's face light up as he unwrapped a new toy and thought about how Jesus brought joy to everyone who believed in Him.

When all the gifts were opened, Abby had an idea. "What if we take some of these cookies to Mrs. Carter?" she suggested. "And maybe we can sing her a Christmas carol. I think she'd like that."

Her mom smiled. "That's a wonderful idea, Abby."

THAT AFTERNOON, THE family bundled up and walked to Mrs. Carter's house, carrying a plate of cookies and a small poinsettia. Mrs. Carter, an elderly woman who lived alone, opened the door with a surprised smile.

"Merry Christmas!" Abby said, handing her the cookies. "We wanted to share some Christmas joy with you."

Before Mrs. Carter could respond, Ben started singing "Silent Night," and the rest of the family joined in. Mrs. Carter's eyes filled with tears as she listened, her hands clasped tightly around the poinsettia.

"You've made my Christmas so special," she said when they finished. "Thank you for reminding me of what this day is truly about."

AS THEY WALKED BACK home, Abby felt a warmth in her heart that had nothing to do with the scarves and gloves she wore. Sharing the love of Jesus felt better than any gift she had received that morning. She realized that the joy of Christmas wasn't just about receiving—it was about giving, just as God had given His Son.

THAT EVENING, AS THE family gathered for their Christmas dinner, her dad asked Abby to say grace. She folded her hands and bowed her head, her voice steady and full of gratitude.

"Dear God, thank You for the gift of Jesus. Thank You for loving us so much that You sent Him to save us. Help us to remember that He is the greatest gift and to share His love with everyone around us. Amen."

LATER THAT NIGHT, AS Abby lay in bed, she thought about the day. The presents had been fun, the cookies delicious, and the carols heartwarming, but what stood out most was the quiet joy of knowing Jesus. His love was a gift she could carry with her every day, not just at Christmas.

Before drifting off to sleep, Abby whispered a final prayer. "Thank You, God, for Jesus. He really is the greatest gift."

Conclusion

As the final chapter of "The Children Who Found Christmas" closes, Abby, Luke, Sarah, and Jonah gather once more in their grandfather's warm living room, their hearts full of wonder and joy. Over the past days, they've explored the story of Christmas—not just the manger and the star, but the prophecies, promises, and the incredible love of God that brought Jesus to earth. They've discovered that Christmas isn't just a celebration of the past; it's a call to live differently in the present and to carry the message of Jesus into the future.

Through Grandpa James's stories and the lessons they've learned, the children now understand that Christmas begins with God's promise: a Savior who would come to bring light to a dark world and peace to troubled hearts (Isaiah 9:6). They've seen how Jesus, born in a humble stable, reminds us that God's love is for everyone, no matter how small, ordinary, or forgotten we might feel. And they've felt the joy of the angels, the faith of the shepherds, and the devotion of the wise men, who all point us back to Jesus as the greatest gift ever given.

But as Abby looks at her friends, she realizes something important—this story doesn't end here. "What happens next?" she asks. Grandpa smiles, his blue eyes sparkling. "What happens next, my dear Abby, is up to you." He closes his well-worn Bible and leans forward, his voice warm and full of encouragement. "The story of Christmas didn't end in Bethlehem or with the gifts of the wise men. It continues in the hearts of everyone who believes in Jesus and chooses to live like Him."

Luke's eyes widen. "So... we're part of the story?"

"Yes," Grandpa says with a nod. "You're part of God's story. Just like the shepherds shared the good news they heard from the angels, you can share the joy of Christmas with others. Just like the wise men gave their treasures to Jesus, you can give your time, kindness, and love to those in need. And just as Jesus brought peace, hope, and light into the world, you can shine His light wherever you go."

Sarah speaks softly, her voice full of wonder. "It's like Christmas isn't just a day. It's something we live every day."

"That's exactly right," Grandpa says. "Being a Christian means living out the message of Christmas all year long. It means remembering that Jesus is always with us—Immanuel, God with us—and letting His love guide everything we do."

As the fire crackles in the hearth and the snow falls softly outside, the children sit quietly, each one thinking about how they can carry the spirit of Christmas into their lives. Abby decides she'll be more patient with her little brother. Luke promises to help their elderly neighbor shovel snow. Sarah plans to write notes of encouragement to her classmates, and Jonah whispers that he'll pray for his friend who feels lonely.

Grandpa smiles, watching their young faces glow with determination and love. "And remember," he says, "you're not doing this alone. Jesus is always with you, helping you, guiding you, and giving you the strength to share His love."

As they say goodnight and head to bed, the children feel a sense of peace that has nothing to do with gifts or decorations. They've found Christmas—not just in the story of Jesus' birth, but in the way it calls them to live. They've learned that being part of God's story means sharing His light, trusting His promises, and loving others with the same grace He has shown them.

And so, "The Children Who Found Christmas" ends where it began—with the promise of hope, the joy of salvation, and the assurance that God's love is always with us. Yet, it's not an ending at all, but a beginning. For every reader who turns these pages, the same call remains: to live the story of Christmas, to shine the light of Christ, and to carry His peace into a world that so desperately needs it.

Now it's your turn. The story continues with you. Will you take the joy of Christmas and share it? Will you let the Prince of Peace guide your steps and bring His love to others? If so, then you, too, have found Christmas—and its meaning will live in your heart forever.

Don't miss out!

Visit the website below and you can sign up to receive emails whenever Joshua Rhoades publishes a new book. There's no charge and no obligation.

https://books2read.com/r/B-A-AJLBB-SSTIF

Did you love *The Children Who Found Christmas*? Then you should read *A Christmas Journey of Faith*[1] by Joshua Rhoades!

[2]

In "A Christmas Journey of Faith", join four friends—Jake, Emma, Max, and Maya—on a thrilling time-travel adventure. When they discover a mysterious time machine hidden in an old shed, they embark on an incredible journey that takes them over 2,000 years into the past to witness the most important event in history: the birth of Jesus Christ. But this journey isn't just about seeing the past—it's about learning timeless lessons of faith, trust, and courage.

As they travel back to the time of Mary and Joseph, the friends witness the Christmas story unfold. From the angel Gabriel's visit to Mary to the long journey to Bethlehem and the miraculous birth of Jesus in a humble stable, they find themselves in the heart of the greatest miracle. They stand in awe as the shepherds receive the good news from the angels, follow the star with the wise men, and learn how Mary and Joseph trusted God's plan, even when it was difficult.

---

1. https://books2read.com/u/bWA9Qz

2. https://books2read.com/u/bWA9Qz

Each step of their journey shows how faith in God can guide us through life's challenges. The friends learn that Christmas isn't about presents or decorations, but about the gift of Jesus, who came to bring peace, love, and hope to the world. As they experience these incredible events, they realize that God's love and salvation are for everyone—rich or poor, young or old.

"A Christmas Journey of Faith" is a heartwarming story that reminds readers of all ages to trust God's plan and embrace the true meaning of Christmas. Through the eyes of Jake, Emma, Max, and Maya, readers will be inspired to live out the message of salvation and faith that Jesus brought to the world.